A Compass for Healing

^A Compass for Healing

Finding Your Way from
Emotional Pain to Peace

Noah benShea

Health Communications, Inc.
Deerfield Beach, Florida

www.hcibooks.com

Library of Congress Cataloging-in-Publication Data

BenShea, Noah.

A Compass for healing : finding your way from emotional pain to peace / Noah BenShea.

p. cm.

ISBN 13: 978-0-7573-0558-0 (Trade paper)

ISBN 10: 0-7573-0558-X (Trade paper)

1. Peace of mind.   2. Conduct of life.   3. Mental healing.   I. Title

BF637.P3B46 2006

158.1—dc22

2006028749

HCI, its Logos and Marks are trademarks of Health Communications, Inc.

Publisher: Health Communications, Inc.
3201 S.W. 15th Street
Deerfield Beach, FL 33442–8190

Cover and inside photos ©Geoff Delderfield and ©Comstock Images
Cover and inside book design by Lawna Patterson Oldfield

Dedication

Once there was an elderly widow who had been diagnosed with an illness that gave her only a brief time to live. Determined to get her affairs in order, she contacted her late husband's best friend and had him come to her house to discuss certain aspects of her final wishes. She told him what music she wanted played at her passing, what passages of her family Bible she would like read, and the special dress she wanted to be buried in. The woman also asked to be buried with her scrapbook of family memories. Just as everything appeared to be in order, and as the friend was preparing to leave, the woman suddenly remembered something very important to her. "There's one more thing," she said, with her well-known spirit of determination.

"What's that?" asked the friend.

"This is very important," the woman continued, her voice well paced, "I want to be buried with a fork in my right hand."

The friend stood looking at the woman, his mouth agape, unsure if he should say anything.

"Have I caught you by surprise?" The woman chuckled.

"Well, in all candor, yes, yes, you have," answered the friend.

The woman's explanation was now as patient as her planning. "In all my years of attending meetings of the botanical gardens, socials, fund-raisers and community dinners, I always remember that as the dishes of the main course were being cleared, another woman would almost always come over and whisper in my ear, 'Keep your fork.' And when I heard that, a smile would almost burst my heart because I could tell that something better was coming . . . like angel food cake with strawberry sauce, or fresh peach cobbler, or something decadent with chocolate, but whatever it would be, I just knew it would be great!

"So, I just want people to see me there in that casket with a fork in my hand and I want them to wonder 'What's with the fork?' Then I want you to tell them that I said: 'Hold on to your forks . . . the best is yet to come.'"

Dear Reader,

This book is dedicated to all of you, who will, with courage and faith, hold on to your forks and realize that the best is yet to come.

Contents

Contents

Prologue

If you looked in the pocket of a wealthy European in the eighteenth century, you would most likely find not one but two pocket watches. The reason is that pocket watches at that stage in their evolution were inclined to run down, and you had no way of knowing when a watch would stop running. Consequently, when a watch ran down you would use the other watch to reset its mate.

As human beings we are not so dissimilar. Each of us is at some point going to run down, need to stop and reset ourselves with someone else's help. And no one who is approached for help should ever feel superior at that time, because at some point that helper will also run down and need a friend.

Feeling emotionally lost, feeling a need to reset ourselves and feeling emotional pain are all part of the human experience, a part of the human linkage of one to another. We all count and count on one another.

Introduction

In this challenging and changing world we all have emotional pain. For any of us trying to avoid or work our way out of emotional pain, here is a Compass to help us find our way with ourselves, with others and with any issue we may face.

We are all circumscribed
by our mortality. We all belong
to one tribe, the tribe of time
and vulnerability. What makes us
all blood brothers and sisters
is that we all bleed. If you cut
any of us just below the surface,
you will find all of us.

Even emotionally healthy people experience emotional pain. Because everyone has some emotional pain, and because everyone touches the lives of others, this book is about emotional healing for all of us. And as there are no strangers to emotional pain, and because nothing feels better than the lessening of pain, I have tried to write this book as if I was talking with a friend—a friend I want to be less often in pain, more often at peace.

My commitment in this book is to help you so that your past pain does not become a self-fulfilling prophecy, that your old hurts do not become your future wounds, that you do not make your fears your fate and that your past does not kidnap your future.

If you want to move from emotional pain to peace, and if you have the courage and the will to make this journey, here is a *Compass for Healing* that is within your grasp. This new Compass and its timeless lessons will absolutely help you find your way.

1

What Is the Compass?

Information is power, and the Compass is a source of power that puts vital information at your service. This power can put you in charge of your life and change your life.

The Compass is not intended to replace common sense, or a life and love of learning, or a spiritual ally such as prayer. Like any tool, the Compass works once you learn how to use it. It won't take you long, but it will take you a long way. The Compass will show you the right way, and it will help you leave your pain behind right away. The Compass isn't a device. It is a guide. It is a way of looking, thinking, acting and reacting.

Most of us live our lives in states of reaction to an unexpected pain that came knocking at our door. But we are certainly better served if we can be pro-active in finding peace.

The Compass will help you send out an invitation so peace will feel welcome at your table. It will help you set a place for peace at your table, and it will help you find a way to show pain the door.

The heroic dignity of life is in how we deal with the day–to-day. No less important is our decision to find a way to make each day a day during which we leave pain further behind and bring peace another step closer. On all these issues, the *Compass for Healing* will help you find your way.

How This Compass Came About

Things don't have to be good for us to be great, and often the really good things that happen to us in life aren't seen to be positive when they happen. Good things can appear as only a passing experience, or even something painfully negative.

The Compass came about because of two different experiences that I like to think crossed my path, but I may have run into them. I'd like to tell you that I knew what was going to happen when I came heart to heart with these experiences or that I was intellectually prepared for them, but I didn't, and I wasn't. The philosopher Sartre had it right: "Life is lived forwards and understood backwards." And the time in between, when we're caught looking backward at a life going forward, can be damned uncomfortable.

So let me go backward for a moment and share what happened. Part one of the story goes like this:

We all live on a little blue ball spinning in space at approximately one thousand miles an hour. Finding our balance is not something any of us can ever fully achieve. It is 24/7/365 work. We can find our balance at any moment and lose our balance the next.

"God made the world round so we would never be able to see too far down the road."

—Isak Dinesen

In my own life, after a lifetime of writing and thinking and addressing others on finding their way, I hit a period when I found myself in the emotional high seas of a long-term marriage that was ending, and I was uncertain, to say the least, about how to find my own way with myself, my former wife and my kids. I was suffering from a very real fear of drowning in emotional pain and not knowing where to row or toward what lighthouse I should go.

In the middle of those dark nights, I was clearly confused and in pain. While I thought I understood what had happened—the he said–she said, you did–you didn't—one of the most familiar mistakes that happens to people in pain is to confuse knowing what happened to them with getting better or being healed. Finding clarity in the past is not the same as finding the path ahead. Knowing where we were yesterday may be reassuring, but it is not necessarily a path for finding our way tomorrow. Old dialogues and old scripts could only tell me what to say and where to stand in a world that was no longer standing or, worse yet, might have led me deeper into the mess in which I found myself.

My situation and my own personal history were akin to the citizens of a town hearing that a terrible flood was coming in three minutes. Some of the people gave up and prepared to drown, and some of the people said prayers. But a few folks decided they had two minutes left, and they had better use that time to learn how to live under water. And that was also my decision. The problem was, I didn't know how to do that.

While the scenario I just described was playing in my life, concurrently, part two of the story goes like this:

Over the last number of years and particularly in light of the emotional distress I was experiencing, I have made several trips to Italy and in particular to a picturesque and historic region called the Amalfi coast. The best way, certainly the most beautiful way, for me to make this journey has been to take a boat from Naples or Capri, arriving in time for the sunset.

I usually stay at the Villa Maria in Ravello, which rests on the hills above Amalfi, and then take a small bus down to visit the ancient seaside city to walk in the sea at the end of the day or for dinner.

On one of these end-of-the-day visits to Amalfi, and as the day's heat began to dissipate, somehow in the town square I noticed a statue I must have passed twenty times yet had never seen. Here was a large and very old bronze-turned-green statue of Flavio Gioia, the man who, Italian legend has it, was the father of the modern compass. The statue started me thinking, and some research in local libraries in my halting Italian pushed my thoughts down this particular path:

We have now had the benefit of a rather sophisticated compass for over five hundred years, and yet even now, so long after the invention of the compass, who among us has not felt lost in life or feared we were losing it—myself included?

Who among us has not felt afraid of losing his or her way in the day-to-day, or in the dark, or in love, or at work, or in growing up, or in growing older?

Who among us has not felt afraid of losing the company of others, or having only our own company, or wondering who could possibly want our company?

How many among us have fears that we have lost

our way or could lose our way in alcohol, drugs, gambling, food, failure, purchasing or pursuing success?

Historically, in an attempt to find their way, people have turned from reading trail signs to the stars to maps and eventually, thankfully, to a compass. All of these earliest methods helped those who were lost find their way or stay on track. However, though most of us these days can tell north from south, we still need to find our way . . . all of us, including me.

And then it hit me.

Like those who came before me, I needed a compass, not a map. A map could mostly show me where I had been but not point me toward the new realities of new worlds that were unfolding overnight and in my soul's dark night.

I also knew that I wasn't lost geographically but emotionally. I needed not just any compass; I needed a new kind of compass.

This book describes the compass I created to meet that need. And, in creating a compass to speak to my own pain, I woke up to realize that I was also addressing the pain that a lot of us in the human neighborhood also experience. We are all alone together, and I was not the only one waking in the night with a fear of imminent floods.

Slowly—over three, four, five years—I began to work my ideas for a new Compass into the seminars, college courses and keynote addresses I was invited to give; into shared conversations with people who were going through tough times; and in my role as advisor to the über-wealthy and powerful, who are caught in pain as often as the rest of us. And the Compass worked. People got it, fast.

Now, after further reflection and almost nine years later, I can testify that this incredibly simple concept connected to timeless wisdom can make and has made a very real difference in the lives of many. The lab work for this Compass was done in the middle of very real lives, including my own. This Compass allowed me and others to find our way from emotional pain to peace, not just in dealing with the past, but with the present and all the new stuff that the day-to-day brings, because life is always throwing something else at us just when we feel triumphant about the past and present.

Life is not always wonderful, but it is wonder-filled. My inspiration for the Compass was emotional pain and a trip to the Amalfi coast. When these two experiences met a leap of imagination and a lifetime's work, I learned that the Compass works and will work for you. Today, after nights that knew no end and more than my share of weepings at 3 AM, I know this to be true.

How the Compass Works

The advent of the traditional compass was a huge leap in finding one's way geographically. But the world has changed, and many of us who know where the sun rises and sets still feel lost on many issues and still try—often for a long time and often frustratingly—to find our way emotionally from pain to peace.

The governing principles of the Compass work on the same conditions as the traditional compass. The traditional compass is premised on a magnetized needle always pointing to magnetic north. Only when we can establish where magnetic north is can we establish what is east, south or west. Absent of magnetic north, neither east, south nor west have meaning. They only exist as they exist in relationship. Without magnetic north we are lost. Only when we can establish north can we find our way to anywhere we want to go geographically.

Similarly, with the Compass for Healing we also have to begin with establishing where North is. Once we have done that, we can locate East, South and West and keep from getting lost.* The Compass for Healing, borrowing on wisdom from all cultures across time, offers a new directional matrix based on Humility, Honesty, Love and Faith, and throws a whole new light on how to find our way.

On the Compass for Healing the four historic geographic directions are replaced with guiding stars that offer the following directional beacons:

---

*In this book, capital letters are used to describe elements of the Compass for Healing: East, West, North and South and their accompanying concepts.

North is replaced with **Humility.**

East is replaced with **Honesty.**

South is replaced with **Love.**

West is replaced with **Faith.**

HUMILITY

FAITH   HONESTY

LOVE

North is **HUMILITY** because Humility needs to be our North Star—the unfailing star on which to base a journey, because pride goeth before a fall.

East is **HONESTY** because the sun rising in the east is a truth that cannot be denied, and the truth shall set you free even as humility picks the lock.

South is **LOVE** because Love is passion and compassion, and the heat of the south fuels us for work, pleasures and the pleasure of caring in life.

West is **FAITH** because even when the sun sets in the west we do not lose faith that it will rise again in all its glory, and so shall we, with faith in ourselves and others.

Here is another way to look at how the Compass works and how it can work for you. Think of your eyes as a camera and each of the directions on the Compass as a series of lenses that fit one on top of the other, bringing your vision into sharper and sharper focus so you can find your way from emotional pain to peace and to keep from getting lost. If one of the lenses is absent or dirty, your vision, the picture you see of the world—your world—will be absent or cloudy.

In your life, if you are humble but not honest, or if you are loving but don't have faith in your partner, you will get lost somewhere along the way. The

Compass keeps us on track. It reminds us that any issue of character on the directional matrix that is unaddressed or abandoned will require a revisit, a reexamination so that you can keep on track.

When the ancient compass was discovered, anyone who had the resources to have one considered themselves blessed because they knew the consequences of not having a compass.

Once you decide you want to go from emotional pain to peace, you can stop at any moment in your day or night, anywhere along the way, and take a reading on how you are interacting with the four vital character issues on the Compass for Healing. If you don't pay attention to how you are doing or where you are going in any of these four areas, you will definitely pay later—and may indeed be paying right now.

This wisdom, this character and directional matrix, and the compass points of Humility, Honesty, Love and Faith emerge from common sense and our common experience. They do not conflict with any major religion or belief system; actually they echo the basis of almost every belief system from Buddhism to Alcoholics Anonymous, from Islam to IBM, from Kabbalah to Christianity, from Taoism's Wei Wu Wei to Weight Watchers. Though I have provided the matrix from these compass points, the wisdom isn't mine. It is ours. It is *yours*, if you will claim it for your life, if you want to move from emotional pain to peace.

If you wonder why this concept isn't more complicated, remember that the obvious is often camouflaged by its obviousness.

Two Things You Need to Know to Begin Your Healing

Alexander the Great conquered the world, and his teacher was Aristotle. Aristotle's first lesson for Alexander was the same lesson we all need to learn: no one can conquer the world—or their pain—until they are more often self-empowering and less often self-victimizing.

Emotional health does not come without emotional pain. Your pain is part of who you are. You

can't treat your pain if you see
it as an alien living inside of
you. Pain is a legitimate part
of your emotional structure
and in its initial formation

> The road ahead
> is always under
> construction.

may have been an entirely healthy reaction. It is
pain, or the fear of it, that causes us to pull our
hands away from a fire. The difference is that now—
hopefully—you are ready to move away from where
you were to where you want to be.

How the Compass Can Help You

Whether your hurt is new or historic, whether you
are hurting from a relationship that ended or because
you can't seem to make a relationship work, whether
your pain comes from how you feel about yourself or
how others have told you they feel about you, most
of the pain we experience in life comes from being in
a state of confusion. In answer to that confusion, the
Compass for Healing, like the historic compass, will

help you find your way. When you focus on Humility, Honesty, Love and Faith, the Compass allows you to see things inside and outside yourself more clearly than you have in the past and also how you can redirect your future. Simply by focusing on how Humility, Honesty, Love and Faith interact in your life, you can stop going in circles. If you're tired of the pain of confusion, here is a tried and true Compass to help you find your way to peace. It is a gift to those who will hold to it. Finding our way from pain to peace is honorable work in any of our lives. And in every life, it is a work in progress.

Reality is only a memory
ahead of its time.

On every beach there is
always another wave.

Change is the only constant.

At its very foundation the Compass for Healing is designed to help turn you into your own best friend and help you deal with self-destructive behavior that you may have inherited honestly but which is causing too much pain to support, and certainly a behavior that isn't supporting you.

---

*Don't allow your past to
kidnap your future.*

You only have two arms. If you are embracing the past you can't hug the future—or yourself. The Compass will help you see where you are getting caught and show how to catch a ride on the river to emotional peace.

If you're tired of rowing, here's a chance to steer.

2

Humility:
The Northern Star
on the Compass

A man was chosen the humblest man in his community by members of his church and was given a pin to represent the honor. The following Sunday he wore the pin to church, and it was taken away from him for being proud. The word "humility" can be a confusing term so let us, as we begin, look back to how the word began.

At its earliest root the word "humility" comes from the Latin for "humus," which means soil. And anyone who has ever planted a garden can tell you that humus is the richest ground to grow in, so "humility" implies quite literally to be grounded and nourished so we can reach our heights, our potential. And Humility is North on the Compass for Healing because none of us can find peace or grow Honest, Loving, or with Faith unless we are planted in Humility. After World War II, Winston

Churchill, in all humility, said, "I was not the lion, but it fell to me to give the lion's roar."

Humility is not denying the power you have, nor denying that the power you have may not come from you but through you.

Gaining Clarity

Humility is the Northern star on the Compass because our work on humility, the quieting of one's ego, provides our first step to gaining clarity so we can find our way from emotional pain to peace.

---

*Little is as blinding
as our pride, and so it is
no wonder that pride comes
before a fall. Any of us who are
tired of falling into emotional
pain need to first look at
where pride trips us up
and puts us in pain.*

"Humility," wrote Confucius twenty-five hundred years ago, "is the foundation of all the other virtues."

The ego is the biggest swamp, the deadliest quicksand on the journey from pain to peace. Only when we have calmed our ego can we get an accurate reading on anything else we are thinking about or hoping to do. While seminal thinkers like Freud and Jung placed a major emphasis on the quicksand of ego and pride, many other belief systems also hold issues of ego as their first point in the attainment of a higher consciousness and greater achievement. Timeless and timely belief systems from Buddhism to the bestselling business book *Good to Great* hold humility as the first step toward enlightenment.

The Colonel

Let us focus for a moment on a colonel in North America's air defense system. He has state-of-the-art equipment that gives him real-time data at 360 degrees so he can see every battlefield with total clarity, an accomplishment resulting from a great deal of money and technology. The colonel lives near the airbase; his wife, who also has a high-level job, drops him off to work in the morning.

One morning on the way to work the colonel and his wife get in a fight. The matter is trivial, but the consequence is not. The colonel's pride is threatened by the argument, and by the time he is dropped off he is boiling mad. When he walks into his office it doesn't matter what honest picture technology and money are showing him. He is furious. He is seeing "red." He is seeing everything through his emotions. His windshield to total information is biased by his anger, the affront to his pride. An old saying goes "If all you have is a hammer, everything looks like a nail." Can you imagine where the colonel's hammer could lead him, and all of us, because of his bruised ego?

It doesn't matter how smart you are if you are blinded by your pride. If you are blinded by pride, you're heading for a fall and the pain that goes with it. So right from the beginning the Northern star's role is to keep your windshield clear of your pride so you can better see where you are heading or why you've been heading in the wrong direction.

If you're one of many who is looking for answers—perhaps as to why your love life (or lack of it) is causing you pain—then beginning at Humility you simply work your way around the Compass, moving from Humility to Honesty to Love, checking to see where you may have lost your way.

On this journey we can acknowledge that anyone caught up in their own pride is not going to be honest, and anyone who can't be honest is going to have trouble in their love life. So if your love life is causing you pain, you might begin not by self-destructively blaming your partner or yourself, but by going backward for a moment and checking your ego, and from there checking your ability to be honest. That doesn't mean just being honest with your partner. It first of all means being honest with yourself about what you're really looking for, what you're really willing to give, whether you're unable to bend your pride or you expect your partner to serve your ego. Since love is made up of both passion and compassion, think about whether your need to be cared for includes your capacity to be caring.

> "Hell is being caught in ego."
> —CARL JUNG

We cannot hope to get to someplace higher or move beyond our pain until we are prepared to acknowledge how far we have to go—and how low we sometimes feel. Consequently it is not surprising to read in Psalm 61:2 "Lead me to a rock that is too high for me."

James and Meredith

James, a bachelor, feels he is in emotional pain because he is alone. When James sees Meredith he wants her to like him. Whenever they're together he tells her about all the great things he has done, and he has accomplished a great deal. Meredith, however, feels overwhelmed, feels like less, and consequently does not think more highly of James.

Let's take another approach. James wants

Meredith to like him. He tells her about all the great things he sees in her. Meredith feels like more and feels even more for James.

James's emotional pain is lessened not by thinking less of himself but by taking the time to think more of Meredith.

In the nineteenth century there were two great British prime ministers, Gladstone and Disraeli. It was said that after you came away from an evening of dining with Prime Minister Gladstone, you felt you had just dined with the wisest person in the empire. But after you came away from an evening with Prime Minister Disraeli, you came away thinking you were the wisest person in the empire.

Feeling Good About Who You Are and Who You Aren't

What matters most is not who matters more but that we all matter. Humility's contagious healing is that feeling good about who we are, not what we are, inevitably takes us to seeing the best in others.

Judaism instructs that the Torah can teach you everything but "fear of God." "Fear of God" isn't about praying to a scary God but acknowledging to the ego that fear is something bigger than us. Until we come to God with humility, we are filled with ourselves. Unfortunately, people who are filled with themselves cannot be increased by others—or by the Divine. Ironically, we can be in pain because we are emotionally starved and yet be filled with ourselves at the same time.

Some years ago I was on a lecture tour with the first American to climb Mount Everest. He told me that other men were constantly coming up to him and wanting to go climbing. To reassure this famous mountaineer about their ability, they repeatedly told him that they were without fear, and he turned them all down. "I couldn't climb with someone who had no fear," said this heroic adventurer. "They will get me killed."

> Pride feeds the ego but starves the soul.

Our pride not only puts what is the best in us at

risk, it also makes others vulnerable. When we look through the lens of Humility, we can look at ourselves without concern for whether we are "more" or "less" but simply as we are and thus afford ourselves a healthy perspective. To do less certainly makes us less and biases our view of others and the world around us.

While we can't always be strong we can still be a source of strength to each other.

"We don't see the world as it is but as we are."

—Anais Nin

Jesus was the "lamb" and a reminder of the power of humility. Only those who can know themselves to be less can become more, and people who see themselves without weakness or people who out of pride refuse to allow others to see their weaknesses are the most vulnerable.

Tom and Lisa

Tom is the son of an uncommunicative father whose notion of the dominant male was suffering and silence. Tom at middle age is now in his own life going through some changes that he is uncertain of, and he is afraid that if he allows his wife, Lisa, to see him in his uncertainty, she will see this as weakness. So he mimics the earliest male model he had and hides in silence. Tom doesn't allow Lisa to really see him, and Lisa relates only to the projected image Tom allows her to see.

Sitting at home that night feeling emotionally isolated, Tom throws himself a pity party. Tom thinks to himself, *Lisa doesn't see the real me*, and sees it as a flaw in Lisa. The relationship flounders, and Tom and Lisa are both in pain.

If Tom had used the Compass to access the courage of Humility, the scenario might have gone like this: Tom is afraid that if he really allows Lisa to see him, she will see this as weakness. So Tom tells that to Lisa. She says she is so glad to hear this because she loves him and also has been going through some things about which she feels vulnerable, and if he could be vulnerable, then she could find the courage to be vulnerable also. On hearing this, Tom begins to feel that even in his vulnerability he can now be protective of Lisa, and Lisa feels the same way—openness prevails; their shared vulnerability is a healthy step toward more peace in themselves and in their home.

Acknowledging That Weakness Is a Strength

"Humility," wrote pastor Harold Warner, "is the gateway into the grace and favor of God." Humility is the gateway to God's healing power. If you want to heal and move from emotional pain to peace, humility is the door to healing.

Strength is not the absence of weakness but how we wrestle with our weaknesses.

Let's look at another Compass heading for a moment and see how Humility and Honesty intertwine in our personal and professional life and how the Compass can help you by witnessing where things go wrong. This time we turn to Joe and Kathy.

Joe and Kathy

Joe is the head of a big company, and the son of a man whose insecurity always made him want to impress others. Joe is married to Kathy, the daughter of a woman whose idea of happiness was always contingent on not saying anything to upset her husband.

The people who work for Joe know that when they come to him with an idea, Joe is more likely to like the idea if he thinks it's his. Joe's pride colors his management style and doesn't allow him to honestly understand that making others more could make him more. It also means that Joe is being cut out of the best ideas that might come his way because Joe can't give anyone else credit. Because people who don't feel appreciated don't care, Joe's company suffers. Joe has to answer for this and has an answer that supports his pride. Joe complains to his superiors about the quality of his staff. When Joe hears the truth from his superiors, he can't be honest with this truth either and feels they also don't appreciate him—making him the victim of his own malaise yet again.

When Joe comes home from work, Kathy can tell he's emotionally upset and wants to know what's wrong. Joe doesn't want Kathy to know what's wrong because then she might honestly see his vulnerability as a human being. So Joe uses emotional distraction by finding something wrong in the way Kathy is doing things at home, hoping the attention will be diverted from his own dishonesty. Kathy can sense this and emotes anger but can't quite get herself to say anything about what's really wrong. In response to Kathy's anger, Joe feels the same way he felt when his superiors chastised him earlier, and like most of us he allows his insecurity to translate as aggression—this time toward Kathy. Joe and Kathy lie in bed at night, feeling caught and in pain, misunderstood and unappreciated.

Joe's inability to access his humility makes it impossible for him to be honest, which makes his pain inevitable. If Joe had looked to the stars of Humility and Honesty to find his way at work and love, he would not be lying in bed grimacing in pain and counting the tiles in the ceiling because he can't sleep. If Joe and Kathy metaphorically had the Compass next to their bed, Joe would see that Kathy was in bed with him looking to have his arms around her just as much as he was in need of being hugged, because life challenges all of us; herein is our shared humanity and shared courage of day-to-day living.

Aspects of Joe and Kathy live in each of us. As you read the chapters ahead, you will discover that no matter what Compass heading you are looking at, it is a mistake to presume that any of the headings—Humility, Honesty, Love or Faith—begins anywhere but with you. You are the ground zero in your life. You are the launching pad for wherever you hope to go.

In Buddhism achieving "nothingness" is the first step in gaining access to everything. "Worship," said the Buddha, "means revering your real self and your humbling delusions."

The Northern star of Humility allows us to honor the true self, not the inflated self, to see the delusions that have kept us as less than we might be making of ourselves, and the emotional pain of living in dissonance from our true self—a reflection of the Cosmic Self of which we are all a part. The Northern star of Humility not only helps us heal our pain of separation from our true self but also heals our rupture from the Divine and the Divine in each of us.

At Alcoholics Anonymous the first of twelve steps begins: "We admitted we were powerless. . . ." There is something bigger than me or my ego, no matter what my ego is telling me. At AA, humility is the first step to healing from the habit and emotional pain of any addiction. One of my favorite quotes borrowed from AA teaching reads, "Humility isn't thinking less of yourself but thinking of yourself less."

Often what blocks our view of the truth and keeps us in pain is our ego standing in front of us disguised as ourselves. Remember Tom in his ego-guise, wondering why Lisa doesn't see the real Tom?

Some might wonder how Humility on the Compass for Healing can be a successful perspective in the winner-takes-all attitude of the business world, where, to borrow from Darwin, "Nature is red in fang and claw." But though the lion may kill to eat, it doesn't take pride in the kill.

Jim Collins, in his *New York Times* business bestseller *Good to Great*, tracks the number-one trait among the best CEOs in America: humility. According to Collins, "[Greatness] means having the humility . . . that will lead you to best possible results." If you want to move from the emotional pain of being less to the peace that comes from being your best, humility is the entrance onto the highway.

You Are the Healer

For many of us who want to move past our emotional pain, the prospect of beginning at Humility seems like a distraction from getting busy and getting going. But sometimes nothing gets us where we want to go faster than stopping what we're doing.

The best way to get where you want to go emotionally is to stop and take a look at where your ego and pride are steering you before you take off anywhere. Too many of us have a "ready, fire, aim" approach to moving from pain to peace.

Let me share with you a story from my book *Jacob the Baker*:

A student was waiting in the rain to seek Jacob's advice. The boy ran alongside Jacob and matched his stride.

"Jacob, what are the limits of a man?"

"Ask the man," said Jacob, without losing his pace.

"And what if the man acknowledges no limits?"

"Then you've discovered his."

"But," the student persisted, "what then is the route to wisdom?"

"Humility!" came the reply.

"How long is the route?"

And Jacob answered, "I don't know."

Hemingway said, "Every great writer must have his own B.S. detector." Every person who wants to be a better person must do the same. Only you will know when you are falsely humble and saying or doing something to feed your pride. The Compass for Healing is designed so you can take an honest reading on you, or give that reading an honest reaction.

Several years ago, Notre Dame's All-American center Frankie Szymanski developed a reputation for his excellence on the football field and his humility everywhere else. Despite accolades from fans and sportswriters, he was never heard to brag or speak highly of his football prowess. During the middle of his senior year, he was called as a character witness for a trial in South Bend. The attorney asked if he was on the Notre Dame football team. Frankie replied that he was. Next the lawyer asked what position he played. "Center," replied Szymanski, without looking up. "How good a center are you?" demanded the attorney.

The shy young man squirmed in his chair but in confident tones answered, "Sir, I am the best center in the history of Notre Dame."

His coach, who was in the courtroom, was

shocked by such a statement from the usually mod-est player. After court was adjourned, the coach asked him why he had made such a statement. Szymanski blushed and responded, "I hated to do it, Coach, but after all, *I was under oath!*"

The Healing Oath

Even when we acknowledge that Humility can be the Northern star in finding our way to move from pain to peace, it can still be a difficult notion to understand.

If the truth shall set us free, humility is the way
to begin picking the lock.
Humility requires me to love myself for my
emotional pain, not in spite of it.
Humility requires me to see myself with clarity
and love myself for this clarity.

---

*"Compassion directed to
oneself is humility."*

—Simone Weil

If humility is compassion directed to oneself, that means we have to love ourselves when we feel foolish, vulnerable, confused or wrong, or when we've been hurt by others.

Humility is the strength to see when we are weak and the courage to embrace ourselves for our vulnerability.

It Is Only a Fool Who Has Never Felt Like One

There was a wonderful teacher three hundred years ago named Nachman of Bratslav who told his students, "Others tell you stories to put you to sleep. I tell you stories to wake you up." I try to take that approach as well.

This story, also from my book *Jacob the Baker*, will perhaps awake inside you an answer to some of your questions.

Once there was a fool who set out for the king's palace. Along the way, people pointed and jeered at him, "Why should a man like you be going to see the king?" they laughed.

"Well, I'm going to be the king's teacher," answered the fool. But his conviction only brought even greater laughter from the people along the path.

When the fool arrived at the palace, the king thought he would make short work and great jest of this man. So, the king had the man immediately brought to the royal court.

"Why do you dare to disturb the king?" demanded his majesty.

"I have come to be the royal teacher," said the fool.

The king twisted with laughter. "How can you, a fool, teach me?"

"You see," said the man, "already you ask me questions."

The king gathered himself and stared at his ridiculous opponent. "You have offered me a clever response, but you have not answered my question."

"Only a fool has all the answers," came the reply.

"But, but," now the king was sputtering, "but what would others say if they knew the king had a fool for a teacher?"

"Better to have a fool for a teacher than a fool for a king," said the man.

When he heard this, the king, who was not a bad man, confessed, "I'm afraid you're right, and now I feel like a fool."

"No," said the man across from him, "it is only a fool who has never felt like one."

"The person who is
afraid to risk failure seldom
has to face success."

—Coach John Wooden

Anyone who has never made a mistake has never made much of anything. We all make mistakes. Let's try to make some new ones.

Keep Your Ego, but Keep It in Check

None of us will lose our egos. Humility isn't about erasing something so vital to our well-being. Our ego serves us in so many ways it is tough to count. But what we need to take count of are the ways that we serve our ego and/or our ego doesn't serve us.

Our ego likes to think it's in control. The more the ego thinks it controls, the more it is inflated. Humility reminds us that there are events and powers outside of us, greater than us, and what should be a source of pride for us is how we respond, not what we control.

The most difficult part of this journey from emotional pain to peace begins with being straight with yourself, which means getting straight with your ego and checking in on your humility.

When you look at Humility on this Compass, use it as a point of orientation so you can separate what you are feeling from who you are and meet yourself face-to-face. Humility's purpose on the Compass is to remind you that you are way more important than your ego's concerns, or your ego's notion of who you should be, or someone else's ego's notion of how you should be, should have been or might yet be. Often these "borrowed feelings" are feelings hoisted on you by those whose own confusion makes them feel better when they're telling you what to feel. When you face these facts you are ready to move farther around the Compass to the other directional markers that will allow you to take the next steps on the journey to peace.

Ego is always
thinking about what others
are thinking of it.

If you want to make it more complicated than it is, more complicated than having the character to get straight with yourself and your pride, then you can. And you can distract yourself with these actions. And you can put off again what you have likely put off over and over again—and put yourself in pain, again.

How You Can
Keep from Returning to
Painful Behavior

As we less often suffer from pride, we can see many reasons that we keep returning to painful behavior. The same mind that allows us to send a man to the moon also likes to send new information down the same canals in our brain where it has sent previous information in the past. So we literally get a kind of mental homesickness when we hear things that challenge or vary from how we have looked at things in the past, even if that way of looking at things has put us in emotional pain and causes us to say we're sick and tired of our way of living.

The lure of the past is magnetic,
and many of us confuse our rut
with a dance floor.

The other side of the "pride trap" is more psychological. No matter what we may think we have in mind for our lives, our egos—imprinted by family, faith, community and experience—have their own scripts in mind. When things don't work out the way the ego wants—when circumstances are not supportive of the ego's imprinted script—then our egos tells us we're not happy and this isn't going to be good for us. Often when things don't work out the way we want, things have in fact worked out for the better but our egos won't hear of it. Sometimes we have to get dragged kicking and screaming to a better place.

Pride is so insidious and sneaky that it can, and will often, take pride in lying to you. So the same way you have to keep reminding yourself about any number of things you have to do in a day, make the Northern star of Humility something you keep an eye on and think about, because getting caught in old traps is something you can mistakenly take pride in and regret later.

Kelly

The major influence in Kelly's life was her grandmother. Kelly's grandmother was a powerful woman who needed to control everyone else. Kelly grew up thinking that if she wasn't perfect she was lacking in character, and Kelly, like her grandmother, took a lot of pride in her character. Other people always seemed to disappoint Kelly. Her pride led to her judgmental personality, and her judgmental personality meant she didn't really have many close friends. Thinking back on her grandmother, Kelly thought about how her grandmother also had few friends because few could survive her pride's scrutiny and the need to find flaws in others to feel better about herself. Thinking on the new

Compass, Kelly realized that her need to be right may not have been the right path to peace. Kelly began to understand that those who always need to be right are usually wrong.

◆ ◆ ◆

Richard

Richard knows he gets victimized by his ego. He has felt the pain of it, and he has gone to great lengths in his relationship with Keri to be his best and not his most inflated self. Leaving home and heading for the gym to work out, Richard soon finds himself circling the parking lot for five minutes trying to find a space. When he finally spots a space, it turns out another person, coming from a different angle, has the same space in mind. Richard goes ballistic, shouting and cursing at the prospect of losing "his" space. The other driver is intimidated and backs off. Richard feels victorious for five seconds and then realizes that this is his old self, the Richard who was a pain to himself and others because he was less than his best self. The new Richard reminds himself that he would not have felt threatened about someone taking "his" place because "his" place in the universe is not a parking place. Thinking on his internal Compass, he resets himself on his path and reminds himself that his feeling better with himself is not in being "master of the parking lot" but his righteous pride in being a good man who is more inclined to giving than taking, who is self- and not other-controlling, who finds strength in being humble within the universe. Richard on reflection realizes that he can be his own teacher and student, and even a parking lot can become a Zen classroom, and a personal awakening to peace can happen at the turn of a steering wheel on the great wheel of life.

Making Sure Your Strengths Are Not a Weakness

While we tend to think that the Northern star of Humility will be an ally to people who feel vulnerable and lack self-esteem, it is just as often, and perhaps more often, an ally to people who feel they are strong, successful, in charge and bubbling with self-esteem. Everything good has a dark side.

In Judo the aim is not necessarily to find your opponent's weakness but his or her strength. In work and love it is often our strengths that throw us.

You had better like your strengths because you are going to pay for them.

To those who at the moment seem to be basking in success and wondering why they, too, need the Compass and to take their bearings from Humility, a few thoughts:

Finding and losing our way emotionally, morally, philosophically, spiritually and/or intellectually is not just something that happens on dark and stormy nights . . . and certainly not just to "others."

Whether we're rich or poor, a bright candle or a dimwit, the ability to become lost is an equal opportunity employer. Success on a bright and sunny day can be no less blinding than trying to operate in a blinding storm. All of us have, at some point, been in the dark—sometimes even at high noon.

For successful people the hardest challenge, and the lesson of Humility, is that you are not in charge. None of us can determine what the emotional world will drop on our doorstep any more than we can determine the headlines of the morning paper. If we allow our emotional state to always be a reaction to what the world drops on our stoop, then we will live the emotional life of a pool ball waiting for the next ball to hit it and wondering into what emotional hole we will be dropped.

*The most common pain
in the life of successful people
is the pain that comes from
the ego confusion that correlates
being successful with
being in control.*

While we are not in charge of the universe, one of the most common confusions and profound lessons of Humility is that it is not an excuse. Being humble does not mean you are not accountable.

While you are not in charge of the world, you are in charge of you. You are not in charge of the emotions of others; you are in charge of your emotional response.

Humility Is the Highest Form of Responsibility

Humility doesn't alleviate any responsibility, including the responsibility not to inflate yourself. Exercising that responsibility we can eliminate the pains we suffer from doing just that.

Who you are in your own estimation, how you choose to conduct yourself within yourself and with others, how you choose to emotionally respond to yourself and others is your work.

When they asked Michelangelo how he sculpted the statue of David, he answered, "All I did was chip away the parts that didn't belong."

Humility is the tool that can help any of us begin to chip away the pride parts that are holding us in pain and keeping us from becoming a work of art.

To see the truth we only have to go in search of our blindness.

To hear the truth we only have to listen for our deafness.

To know the truth we only have to learn of our ignorance.

Three Good Questions to Ask Yourself When You Look at Humility on Your Compass

1. Am I doing what I am doing because I think it is the right thing to do or because of how I think others will feel about me?

2. Am I worrying about what's bothering me because I am worried about what others will think of me?

3. What am I afraid to do because of the opinion others will have of me?

HUMILITY

Some Healing Thoughts to Hold in Mind Under the Northern Star of Humility

Few of us have a problem acknowledging that humanity has not yet reached its highest level. If we can also admit this about ourselves, we are already evolving in the right direction.

➤ Admit when some aspect of your life is out of control, and watch yourself take control.

➤ Admit what is not flattering about you. Flatter yourself by admitting it.

➤ Don't confuse being made in God's image with being God.

➤ Don't exercise power just because you can.

➤ All of us are from the hand of God; none of us are the hand.

➤ Laugh when you trip over your own pride.

➤ Openly admire the humility in others.

➤ Embrace what you like least about yourself. Make it yours, and you will make it better.

➤ Ask God how to mine your mistakes. Begin by mentioning them.

➤ Admit to God what God already knows about you.

➤ Do something nice for someone else, and don't tell anyone.

➤ Don't put off accepting yourself until you're perfect. Accept who you are for who you are now, and you will be better off now . . . and have a better chance of being a better you in the future.

3

Honesty:
The Eastern Star
on the Compass

"I am different from Washington," wrote Mark Twain. "I have a higher, grander principle. Washington could not tell a lie. I can lie—but I won't."

Honesty is the root of Twain's observation and commitment. The commitment, however, to be brutally honest with ourselves and others is not an excuse to be brutal. There are all kinds of honesty, and often, kindness is the truest.

Honesty as an Operating Manual for the Planet Earth

"All knowledge begins with honesty."

—Plato

None of us are grown-ups; all of us are growing-ups. No matter our age, our capacity for learning is directly linked to our capacity for honesty. No matter what we want to know, and certainly if we want to know how to find our way from pain to peace, honesty is a guiding principle. People who are lying to themselves about who they are, where they want to go, where they think they are heading or what's bothering them are soon going to find themselves lost and in the emotional pain of feeling lost. Indeed, any of us who are lying to ourselves have already lost our way.

> *"To make your*
> *children capable of honesty*
> *is the beginning of*
> *education."*
>
> —John Ruskin

A little earlier we were talking about the difficulty in grasping humility, but if we thought that humility was a slippery notion, dishonesty is a banana peel we throw in our own path. The truth is that most of us decide what lies we want to believe, and we often do this because of what our egos decide we need to believe. The reason our egos often decide that we need to believe some self-supporting or self-promoting lie is to prop up our needed notion of ourselves. You can see why we can't get to Honesty on the Compass until we find our way through Humility. Humility and Honesty are the midwives to finding our way if we are going to give birth to our best.

"Liars can be honest to themselves just as people who pride themselves in their honesty can lie to themselves. I always divide people into two groups: Those who live by what they know to be a lie, and those who believe, falsely, to be the truth."

—Christopher Hampton

Some people think of "honesty" as a term so common that of course, it has no real transforming and healing capacity.

To this dismissal of Honesty's vital role as one of the four stars by which to guide one's life, I have only one response: If honesty is so simple, why does it seem to cause so many of us so much trouble? If you wonder about the power of honesty, perhaps think instead about the destructive power of dishonesty.

"Thou shall not lie" is one of the Ten Commandments. I tend to see these ten reminders as instructions in an operating manual for life on planet Earth. Of course, some people don't do instructions. And of course, a lot of people are in pain.

No one would knowingly go to a dishonest physician. Any of us really interested in self-healing might remember the suggestion: Physician heal thyself. For both the patient and healer within us, honesty is the byword.

---

*The truth is seldom
hidden but often
overlooked.*

The Honest Path to Peace

*Your honesty won't
necessarily make you a hero
except to yourself.*

An elderly gentleman of eighty-five feared that his wife was growing hard of hearing, so he called her doctor to make an appointment to have her hearing checked.

The doctor made an appointment to test the wife's hearing in two weeks, but in the meanwhile the doctor suggested an informal test so the physician could have a better idea of the problem.

"Here's what you do," said the doctor. "Start out about forty feet away from her, and in a normal conversational speaking tone see if she hears you. If not, go to thirty feet, then twenty feet, and so on until you get a response."

That evening, the wife is in the kitchen cooking dinner, and the husband's in the living room. *I'm about forty feet away,* he says to himself, *so let's see what happens.*

Then in a normal tone he asks, "Honey, what's for supper?" No response.

So the husband moves to the other end of the room, about thirty feet from his wife and repeats, "Honey, what's for supper?" Still no response.

Next he moves into the dining room where he is about twenty feet from his wife and asks, "Honey, what's for supper?" Again he gets no response, so he walks up to the kitchen door, only ten feet away.

"Honey, what's for supper?"

Again there is no response, so finally he walks right up behind her, and asks, "Honey, what's for supper?"

"Damn it, Phil!" shouts the wife. "For the fifth time, we're having CHICKEN!"

> *Often the only thing*
> *we'll avoid more than a bad*
> *mirror is a good one.*

The man in the story has no problem being honest about what he thinks is his wife's condition. His problem is in being honest with himself. Absent of honesty there is nothing he can do to heal the real problem. Until we're prepared to be honest with ourselves, we'll be deaf to what ails us.

Inevitably dishonesty does us a disservice. Little brings us more pain in life than living with a lie. You don't have to be the central character in *Crime and Punishment* to know this agony. While there may be the pain we are causing others by lying, the real question is: what's the painful attraction that caused us to be in denial of the truth?

The allure of the lie is the lure of being in less pain by being dishonest than by telling the truth. Honesty isn't the easy path, but it is the path to

making peace with yourself and healing yourself—
just as being dishonest is the easiest way to lose your
way.

---

*"Far more critical than
what we know or don't know
is what we do not
want to know."*

—Eric Hoffer

On the path to peace, honesty isn't a goal but how
we must travel. Those who tell you anything different are lying, and in lying to you they are trying to
sell the lie to themselves.

Speak Truth to the Power of Denial

A character in the movie *American Beauty* advises
another to never underestimate the power of denial.

On first blush this advice suggests that we bear witness to how much we are capable of denying. On reflection, this advice reminds us never to underestimate the volcanic power that can explode when we are in denial of the truth. On the Compass, the Eastern star of Honesty requires us to be an honest witness not only to where we are heading, and how honestly we are traveling, but also to the implications of our dishonesty.

Frank and Penny

Frank has a weight problem, but he has a bigger problem with being honest about the problem. Frank tells Penny he is going out to get a paper. Penny finds this odd because Frank never goes out to get the paper but denies to herself for the moment that anything is wrong. Frank does get a paper but only to cover up his trip to a fast-food joint, something that Penny would tell him is a bad idea considering the pounds the doctor says Frank needs to lose. Frank doesn't want to be honest about the need to lose the weight. Penny doesn't want to face the lie she knows Frank is telling her and begins to wonder how big the lie is. The pain Frank feels for being dishonest with Penny is nothing compared to the unaddressed pain Frank is feeling because he can't be honest with himself about his weight, getting older, and the threat of diabetes and a heart attack. Penny still wonders about the size of her husband's lie— and also whether Frank is meeting someone and if it is because he finds her less attractive because she is getting older.

When we lie to ourselves and others, the thing we are lying about is almost never "the thing." All the things we are not honestly addressing become a pain, growing in intensity in the shadow of the dishonesty. Lying always leaves collateral damage and wounds that simply binding the lie won't heal and can't heal.

Every private lie becomes a public lie. In the last story, what Frank doesn't want to tell Penny begins with what he doesn't want to tell himself. Triggered by Frank's lie, the haunting fear that Penny doesn't want to hear is filled with its own power. The power of denial is far greater than what we can deny. The power of denial is volcanic; by burying the truth we plant a lie that inevitably grows and with enough neglect blossoms explosively.

---

*"What we refuse
to face becomes
our destiny."*

—Carl Jung

While some of us lie, most of us more often bury the truth rather than distort it. The beauty of the Compass is that if you've visited the Northern star of Humility, you will have less chance of burying the truth out of pride and more chance of visiting it. By visiting the Eastern star of Honesty, you have a better chance of healing than avoiding.

The denial of honesty that we practice in our inner lives will find its role in our personal lives and in our professional lives. The inverse is also true. Practicing self-honesty has a healing role in the living room and the boardroom and with anyone on any issue.

> Honesty is courage in the face of fear and is as capacitating as dishonesty is decapacitating. When we speak truth to power, we empower ourselves.

When we follow the Eastern star of Honesty, we find the truth is its own healing light just as dishonesty will leave us in the dark.

To take a breath we have to release our breath.

How Can You Honestly Find Love

The source of much dishonesty isn't a fear that others will hurt us but that they won't love us. The fear of not being loved is a deep concern because it is connected to a primal fear: the fear of being abandoned. The fear of abandonment is primal fear connected to our caveman beginnings when abandonment meant privation and starvation. This same fear is played out today with all the social nuances of isolation and not fitting in. Dishonesty in the face of this fear seems like the lesser of the two evils—and it would be, if we were still living in caves. But we're not in caves, and personal and social dishonesty often come into play because we're afraid of being alone.

Be honest about
what no longer serves you
and release it.

Fear of being our own company causes much of the personal and social dishonesty that traps us even as we like to think of ourselves as honest. Here's an example: Anyone who has been in a long-term relationship knows that being dishonest is sometimes easier than being disruptive. When a group of long-term married men were asked to name the one trait that kept them married, the overwhelming answer was "acquiescence." "Be like water," said the Buddha. Not needing to be right is often the right way to be right.

But only a fine line separates compromise and dishonesty, and we are often dishonest about that dividing line—not because we want to be like the Buddha, but because we don't want to be caught in this scenario: If I tell the truth, my

We repeatedly fill our lives with little lies in the hope of burying pain. But these tiny lies wake up as the elephant in our living room that cannot be ignored. Unaddressed issues in our lives, like elephants, have long memories and have no trouble finding our address.

significant other may be upset with me, and if my Jack or my Jill is upset with me, he or she may get angry. If they get angry, they may throw me out, and if they throw me out, I'll be alone. And then, and then, and then . . . it dawns on us. I won't be alone. I'll be with me.

Until we can suffer and savor our own company, we cannot suffer and savor the honesty of living honestly. If you find pain in your own company, you will have pain in every relationship. Only when you can honestly make peace with yourself can you honestly hope to find peace with anyone or anywhere.

---

*"When I got off the boat
in Amsterdam, the first person
I met was myself."*

—Voltaire

Honesty Begins at Home

Honesty, like humility, begins at home—with ourselves. Honesty and dishonesty often have nothing to do with other people and everything to do with who we are or need to think we are.

Feeling confused about how to move from pain to peace should never be an embarrassment. Not admitting to one's confusion is the best way to stay lost.

Often we are dishonest because at our core we can't accept who we are. Often we fear our ability to accept ourselves because fundamental to self-acceptance is self-awareness, and too many of us feel that we are a disappointment to our anointed, rather than honest, notion of ourselves.

Real honesty isn't an act and consequently usually plays to very small audiences—often audiences of one. Honestly finding our way with anyone or at any moment isn't a public promotion. The real work in life is often really quiet work.

"Most people find that being themselves is not enough of a show," wrote the American philosopher Mason Cooley. Though I'm not sure most of us feel that way,

I am sure that all of us have felt that way at some time.

All of us have known the feeling of being ourselves and feeling we're not giving others enough of a show to earn their applause. When we grow addicted to the applause, we first grow lonely in its absence, and then grow lonely in its company. Unfortunately the allure of being dishonest, even if it's a source of pain in the long run, is often no competitor to the thought of wild applause in the short run.

Only when we decide to stop being actors and start being who we are can we begin healing the disparity between the two and the inevitable pain that accompanies it.

The Healing Habit of Honesty

Any of us characters who are in character when we strut and fret on life's stage soon discover that most of our insecurities and dishonesties come from needing the applause of others rather than accepting and loving ourselves.

The lies we need to tell become the lies we need. Dishonesty is an addiction, and like most addictions, dishonesty begins as a habit.

When dishonesty becomes a habit, the odds are heightened that it will become an addiction. The best way to break a habit is with another habit. The best way to get out of the habit of lying is by getting into the habit of telling the truth.

Like most actors, most people feel they're not getting the auditions they deserve—the big break they have earned. Because most of us are hoping to play leading roles, we have forgotten that we already play the leading man or leading woman role in our own lives.

Honesty dressed to
make an impression impresses
others as dishonesty.

"Each time an actor acts, he does not hide; he exposes himself," said the actress Jeanne Moreau. She is right. Honesty, as it turns out, has this strange ability to hide us because so many others can't believe that we are hiding in plain sight. In a world where so little is as it appears, little so confuses others like telling them the truth.

What we also tend to forget is that we're not the only ones in hiding. Our dishonesty is something we have to honestly admit we all share and often for the very same, very human reasons.

> Two priests were going on a summer vacation and decided that they would make this a real vacation by not wearing anything that would identify them as clergy.
>
> As soon as the plane landed, they headed for a store and bought some shorts, shirts, sandals, sunglasses and so on.
>
> The next morning they went to the beach, dressed in their "vacation" garb, and were sitting on beach chairs, enjoying a drink, the sunshine and the scenery when a beautiful woman

in a bathing suit came walking straight toward them. They couldn't help but stare, and when she passed them, she smiled and said, "Good morning, Father. Good morning, Father." Nodding and acknowledging each of them individually, she continued on.

The priests didn't know what to say. How could anyone recognize them as clergy?

So, the next day they went back to the store, bought even more pronounced tourist clothing and again went down to the beach.

A little later, the same attractive woman wearing minimal bathing attire came strolling along again.

And again, she approached them and said hello to them: "Good morning, Father. Good morning Father," before walking away.

One of the two clergy couldn't stand it and said. "Just a minute, young woman. Yes, we are priests, and proud of it, but I have to know, how in the world did YOU know?"

"Oh, Father, don't you recognize me? I'm Sister Angela!"

"Give a man a mask,
and he'll tell you
the truth."

—Oscar Wilde

Honesty Alleviates the Fear of Being Discovered for Who You Are

Every part we play in life is only our part at that moment in our lives. When you're a kid, be a kid. When you're an adult, don't kid yourself. Don't get addicted to your role. Roll with it. Honestly accept yourself in whatever role you're in at the moment, and love yourself for not having to play that role when life moves you on to your next part.

Marlon Brando was in an acting class when the direction came for the actors to imagine they were chickens when the air raid siren went off. All the actors but Brando started running around flapping their "wings" and squawking. Brando just sat there. When the instructor asked him why he wasn't doing what the rest were doing, he answered, "I'm a chicken. What's an air raid siren?"

One of the very real ways that the Eastern star of Honesty can help you to diminish pain in your life is by reminding you to play your part in the moment honestly. Play the part and not the result. Our work is not to work at meeting the expectations of others. Charlie Chaplin once won third prize in a Charlie Chaplin look-alike contest.

> A man who spent his whole life attempting to live like Moses expected to be admitted to heaven. When the man's admission was refused, he complained: "I've lived like Moses my whole life."
>
> "Sorry," said the heavenly governing board, "we already had a Moses. We needed you."

We are all gifted because we have all been given the gift of life. Nothing is more painful in life than being dishonest about who you are and spending your life trying to open someone else's gift.

The Honest Power of Self-Acceptance

The honesty of our life experiences requires the honesty of knowing and accepting that we are alone, and that in our aloneness we are brother and sister with all others.

The only thing sadder than spending our lives playing for "Ma" is growing up with no "Ma" to play for. And while we all want to be loved for our performance, Dr. David Richo reminds us, "No one can give you now what you didn't get then."

Falling in love with someone, believing they will love your performance like the "Ma" or the "Pa" you never had, is a show that will have a limited run in any relationship.

Any grown-up actors hoping for a parental audience in a relationship are playing to a parent-child relationship, not an adult-adult relationship. On a very private, insecure and internal stage we're all playing for "Ma" or "Pa" or their absent ghost. But hoping for a partner in life to be the "Ma" or "Pa" giving you the love you never got is dishonest to the adult-adult relationship, and if the partner is coached to play that role, they will eventually be accused by the other with incriminations like "Don't tell me what to do. You're not my father!"

"The reason I'm in this business, I assume all performers are—it's 'Look at me, Ma!' It's acceptance, you know— 'Look at me, Ma, look at me, Ma, look at me, Ma.' And if your mother watches, you'll show off till you're exhausted."

—Lenny Bruce

The Eastern star of Honesty's message is pretty simple: Be honest. Life gives all of us insecurities; the question is what we make of them. Weaknesses are gifts. When we open them we are given strength. Life on and off stage is a judo match. If your opponent is stronger than you, use your weaknesses.

Use the urge to practice dishonesty to fuel honesty by honestly facing your urge to dishonesty. Embrace the urge to be dishonest. Accept it in yourself. To deny it would be dishonest. Be cautious of those who say they are not urged to be dishonest. Actors are born when they step on stage. All of us step on stage beginning the day we're born.

It doesn't matter when we stop believing in Santa Claus. What does matter is when we start honestly believing in ourselves, in our right to be honest and in the honest self we've yet to become.

Some of us look to the stars when we pray. Some of us pray to be stars. The bright lights, however, do not necessarily put us in the spotlight. Rather the absence of light in the cosmos, the surrounding black nothingness of space, makes the smallest star stand out—and reminds us that we are all to some extent in the dark about things. Our dishonesty abounds and makes our smallest honesty glow as a luminous wonder. Use that to guide your life from pain to peace.

Honesty Isn't for the Weakhearted but the Bighearted

Being honest can be scary. Usually we lie because some part of us somewhere is scared of something. Honesty is straight-ahead heroism.

Honesty isn't an easy star to follow, but dishonesty is not a star and will only guide those in search of being lost.

Be cautious of people who have lost their way, who are in pain and who will accuse you of abandoning them if you will not also commit to being

> Codependent sadness is not the same as caring.

lost. People who are not honest about why they are in pain are victimized by the same dishonesty in countless other areas of their lives.

Comedians like to tell the story of the guy who walks into a psychiatrist's office and says:

"I've got a friend who thinks he's a chicken."

"And," asks the doctor, "have you told him that he isn't a chicken?"

"No."

"Why not?"

"Because I need the eggs."

Often the pain in our lives comes from buying into the pain of others and confusing shared reality with reality.

Don't trade the power
to do something about your life
for the self-pity of feeling
sorry for yourself.

"Wound clubs" are popular among those who are committed to ignoring the facts of what happened to them and ignoring the honest opportunity of the new day available to them. The honest truth is that old wounds don't heal when you pick the scabs. And energy given to old wounds precludes using that energy to heal in the present and future. The ability to honestly witness ourselves is necessary to any transformational growth. Until we can step back and take an honest look at who we are and how we've been conducting ourselves, we will be lost in whatever character we have been cast in by the moment or that our egos/fears have cast us in with the hope that we can successfully pull the wool over our own eyes.

Sometimes the smallest truth can be the most difficult for us to access. Sometimes very small truths can seem too big for us to admit, yet as soon as we somehow find the courage to be honest on this tiny issue, we can't believe it took us so long to admit it and how big we made it appear.

Sometimes we have to sneak up on the large truths by getting in the habit of telling small truths. Small truths can be the training wheels we need to learn how to keep our balance. But honesty, like riding a bike, is one of those things that once you learn how to do, you never forget, and losing your balance is just part of the learning.

It takes an honest soul to admit when one's soul is troubled by dishonesty.

HONESTY

Three Good Questions to Ask Yourself When You Look at Honesty on Your Compass

1. Am I telling myself the truth about _____ or is this simply something I am telling myself?

2. Have I been dishonest to myself about _____ in the past?

3. Do I really believe _____ will happen, or am I being dishonest to myself or others because _____?

HONESTY

Some Healing Thoughts to Hold in Mind Under the Eastern Star of Honesty

➤ Being honest is quiet work. Little is as loud as a lie or a liar.

➤ Memory is the gentlest of truths.

➤ The truth is seldom hidden but often overlooked.

➤ Too often when we think we have found the truth, we have only lost our sense of humor.

➤ The truth is like a house where every room has a point of view.

➤ A window is also a mirror; it allows us to look at the world and see ourselves.

➤ We would rather be deceived than rejected, but living with a lie is trading the truth for company.

➤ Don't lie to make people like you.

➤ Don't trade kindness for honesty and think you've made an honest trade.

➤ Don't take credit just because credit lands in your lap.

➤ Observe your intentions and see how they line up against what you tell others is your intent.

➤ Find a mistake you can learn from. Reward yourself by finding another.

➤ Admit to something even if it means you'll get less.

➤ Admit to something you did just so others would think more of you.

➤ Don't confuse being honest with not lying about money or sex. Be honest about lies in other areas of your life and why you lied.

Think about whether what you say is bothering you is what's really bothering you, or are you telling yourself that because you can't admit to something else? Then admit it.

The honesty required to begin the journey from pain to peace is the same honesty that is required for every dishonesty we engender or encounter anywhere on the journey. The lasting truth is that there are no beginnings or endings on life's journey: only markers we declare at random points along the way.

> An elderly couple is sitting at the counter of a diner when the husband turns to his wife and says,
>
> "Look at the couple at the other end of the counter. That's how we're going to look in ten or fifteen years."
>
> The wife laughs.
>
> "What's so funny?" asks the husband.
>
> "That's not another couple," says his wife. "That's a mirror."

In this life, at any moment, there are ten thousand places where honesty can be born, or ten thousand ways it can die.

4

Love:
The Southern Star
on the Compass

What Is Love?

Love is the feeling that we matter.
And if we matter, that others matter.
And without this, nothing matters.
With this, anything is possible.
Without this, nothing is possible.

"Tough love" is a term usually applied to the
need to be straight with someone even when it hurts
them but is necessary for a healing. The reason that
Love is the Southern star and follows the stars of
Humility and Honesty is because it's tough, and perhaps impossible, to be in a loving relationship until
you can calm your pride and be honest. It is amaz-
ing how many people who complain about the pain
of having no love in their lives look everywhere

except whether their own egos and dishonesty have bankrupted their hearts. Others of us, out of our painful personal histories, have created walls to protect our egos, can't be honest with ourselves about the implications of those walls and then blame others for what they won't give us.

Steve and Laurie

Laurie's most common emotional pain complaint is that Steve doesn't love her the way he should. But Steve can only love Laurie the way he can. Laurie would find the same reality with any partner. The relevant question is whether Laurie can love Laurie the way she needs to be loved, but her needs arise from her own self-esteem issues that predate life with Steve. He cannot sort out Laurie's relationship with her ego's needs or what she didn't get once upon a time. Steve has his own work to do, which we see in his complaint about Laurie.

The most common complaint of pain from Steve—and among the Steves of the world—is that Laurie is always telling him what to do. But it doesn't matter what Laurie is telling Steve; it does matter if Steve gives up control and then blames Laurie for taking control. Steve's need to take responsibility for his own life is also a self-esteem issue—an issue of his relationship with his own ego and his own history.

Neither Steve nor Laurie can honestly look at the situation until they can find their way to seeing how their issues of ego are making an honest view hard to come by.

Steve and Laurie need to rise above their egos' temper tantrums and get in touch with really embracing themselves. Only when they have done the uphill work of dealing with their egos' needs (North on the Compass) can they get to honesty (East on the Compass) with themselves and each other, and only then can they honestly have a healthy love relationship (South on the Compass). From there they would move, higher yet, to having faith in who they are and who they are to each other (West on the Compass).

This tango between Steve and Laurie is the most common entanglement of couples who have lost their way with themselves and yet blame their partner. All the Steves and Lauries of the world whose love affairs are in pain need the Compass to find their way out of the woods where they have become lost over a lifetime. This pattern of inherited and learned behavior is negative but familiar and therefore destructively inviting because our brain anatomy loves to run new information down old paths even if it runs us in painful circles.

Love You

Before every airplane flight, the attendant stands up and tells us that should the cabin pressure drop, a mask will fall, and before we do anything for anyone else—even before we put the mask on a vulnerable child or an elderly parent—we are to put the mask on ourselves. Until we take care of ourselves, we can't do anything for anyone.

No one can move from pain to peace who doesn't love themselves enough to make the effort. It is so sad to see people who have disappointed themselves not give themselves exactly what they need to heal, but rather keep giving themselves what has been keeping them in pain.

"Love is an energy which exists of itself. It is its own value."

—Thornton Wilder

Issues of Ego and Dishonesty are highly, highly contagious and infect, not only the person suffering, but also those around them. So as we move around the Compass, we discover that areas that infect the spirit and aren't dealt with, such as pride and dishonesty, soon infect the next Compass heading and turn our experiences of love into experiences of pain.

Bob and Mary

Bob needs Mary's love. Mary can't bring herself to be loving to Bob for any of a thousand "Mary" reasons that have nothing to do with Bob and everything to do with her mother's alcoholism and failed marriage, and a childhood riddled with insecurity that makes giving love risky. Bob feels rejected, which reinforces his childhood pain of a father who made Bob feel he was never good enough, who made Bob feel unworthy and undeserving of love. Bob can't bring himself to give himself what he needs most because his past makes him feel unworthy, and he is further denied in the present because Mary can't give of herself to him. What Mary denies Bob, he denies himself. And what Bob denies himself, he won't be able to give Mary. Their shared pain is cross-reinforced because of the love they can't give themselves.

Many of us never forget to do our exercises or yoga or take a run, but too many of us have long forgotten that the best stretch when you want to leave behind the emotional pain of feeling alone begins by waving good-bye to the past.

Love yourself when you fail,
and you will succeed.

God didn't give us two arms just so we could hold our hands out in expectation of what others will give us. None of us can wrap our arms around the world until we are prepared to give ourselves a hug. So if it has been a long time—maybe too long— since you embraced who you are, do it now, and do it daily.

Love Others

Two Brothers

Once there were two brothers who were
farmers. One of the brothers was married and
lived with his wife and children on one side of
a high mountain. The other brother was not
married and lived by himself on the other side
of the mountain. As it happened, in this year,
there was a harvest of good fortune for both
brothers. But while he slept, the brother who
was married couldn't help but think to himself: *I have my wife and children to help me with
the crops, and my barn is filled. My brother,
however, lives by himself and has no one to help
him. Perhaps he does not have enough. I will
load a wagon with my bounty and carry it to my
brother.*

The brother who lived by himself also could
not sleep. He thought: *My life is blessed. My
crops have been bountiful. My needs are few. My*

brother has a wife and children. He needs more than me. I will load a wagon with my bounty and carry it to my brother.

So with the moon climbing into the night, the brothers loaded their wagons and, each beginning from their side of the mountain, began the ascent. At the top, with the moon now directly overhead, the brothers met. Each immediately understood the intentions of the other, and they fell into each other's arms and cried.

◆ ◆ ◆

A man walking along the shore saw another man drowning only ten feet from shore. The first man threw the drowning man a rope five feet long. When the drowning man expired, the man on shore said, "Hey, it wasn't my fault. I was willing to meet him halfway."

Let us meet one another halfway. Let us worry not only about what's happening to us but think about what's happening to others. Other people aren't here to meet our expectations, but we are. Let us remember that things don't have to be great for us to be great.

Love doesn't just warm
the recipient of your love.
Sometimes the nicest way to get
warm when you're cold is
to hug someone else.

There Is Only Work and Love

It has long been propositioned by the best psychological minds that there is only love and work in life. In other words, only in our resonance with love and work do we come to know who we are.

A man spent his
whole life looking for love
and wandering the world.
Finally, in a fit of despair,
the man turned to the heavens
and asked, "Why me?
Why me?"
And the heavens
answered, "Why not you?
You've looked
everywhere else."

Love not only makes us feel good, but love also is a central experience for us to know who we are. If we come to know ourselves through love, then one can only imagine the pain we would be in if we didn't use the Southern star of Love to help us find our way to peace.

People who are strangers to themselves cannot be people at peace. Coming to know ourselves takes work, but this work also serves our self-examination and self-understanding. The Southern star of Love reminds us that whatever work we are engaged in, we should make it a labor of love.

The dignity of work is not the work but the dignity we bring to the work. Anyone who does not love themselves cannot treat themselves with dignity.

There is an ancient tale of three men sitting cutting stone. Each is asked what he is doing. The first says, "I am making bricks." The second says, "I am also making bricks." But the third says, "I am building a cathedral."

What we do in life, what we make of our life, is mostly determined by the love with which we do it. If you can get past what's in it for you, and if you can't honestly be a part of something greater than yourself, then it will be impossible to open your heart to who you might yet become.

Loving Is Seeing

*Our heart knows what our mind
only thinks it knows.*

You always hear that love is blind, but this does not so much mean that lovers cannot see but that they see with their hearts.

While love is generally envisioned as an act of passion, no less true is that love is also an act of compassion.

Love that is compassionate is not blind at all; it is looking out for others. Remarkably, when we keep a caring eye out for others, we tend to care more for ourselves. The word compassion comes from the Latin and means "with passion."

Compassion is caring with passion.

The mark of a civilization is not classical music, for people have done terrible things while listening to classical music. The mark of a civilization is not porcelain teacups, for people have done terrible things while drinking tea. The mark of a civilization is how people with power act toward people without power. The measure of a civilization is the compassion of people to people.

Using the Southern star of Love, we are reminded to set our sights on being other-compassionate *and* self-compassionate. To move from pain to peace in your life, you have to give yourself the okay to take care of yourself and only from there can you experience the transforming joy of being other-compassionate.

Life is a gift of love.
Loving who we are is a gift to
ourselves. And from there a gift
we can give to others.

Many people are in emotional pain because they have never given themselves the right to take care of themselves, or they were raised to think it was wrong or immoral, or that serving self meant you were not serving others.

Until we can be self-loving we can't be other-loving. And until we can be other-loving we cannot be divinely loved, because God is not blind to how we treat others.

Love Is a Magic Carpet Out of Pain

Love can take you places that reason and logic don't dare travel because it doesn't make any sense for them to go there. While much research shows how prayer can relieve pain, who among us does not know how people in love or people who can access their capacity to love can travel beyond the pain of circumstances?

"Where there is great love there are always miracles."

—Willa Cather

To love and be loved is a miracle. It is a magic carpet that can carry us anywhere. Achieving greatness without loving and being loved—even if that means you can't love an idea—isn't achieving the impossible. It is impossible.

Love is the force that animates life. The force of love does not require something or someone to be the object of affection for love to have its power. Love is its own power and empowers and reminds us that we have the power to move from pain to peace.

---

*"To love a thing means
wanting it to live."*

—Confucius

Many of us feel we are in emotional pain because our lives lack intimacy, but being self-loving requires that we also be self-intimate. This is not something we don't know how to do, but it is something we too often forget to do. Or don't give ourselves the right to do. Or we feel ashamed to do so because we know things about ourselves that make us ashamed. But at some point we all have felt like less. And any of us who are honest know we have at some point let ourselves and others down. The Southern star of Love reminds us that we have told ourselves our deepest secrets and know our fondest hopes and we still need to love who we are. Personal intimacy means we cannot be left alone, only absent the company of others.

Love Is the Company of Solitude

The secret to being loving is hidden in its obviousness. At its root, love is about acceptance. Being loving is welcoming who you are with arms wide open, and being open to who you might yet become.

"Love is, above all, the gift of oneself."

—Jean Anouilh

Loving oneself also requires us to guard our solitude. Honoring who we are does not mean not wanting to be with others. It does mean that we love being at one with who we are.

Lauren and Nick

Lauren feels that Nick doesn't always understand her. And that's okay with her because she knows that she doesn't always understand herself but loves herself even when she confuses herself. Lauren loves the solitude that Nick allows her by not pushing himself to need to understand everything about her. Because of this healthy latitude, Lauren also feels a responsibility to guard Nick's solitude. And Nick loves Lauren for this. Nick still feels that when he sees Lauren she takes his breath away, and he loves her even more because she gives him the room to breathe.

"Love is union with somebody,
or something, outside oneself,
under the condition of retaining
the separateness and integrity
of one's self."

—Eric Fromm

It is not a social sin to be alone. It is a gift because you are a gift to you.

You are a gift that you must love to be loved. Otherwise you are not becoming one with another out of love but joining with another out of a fear of being alone, and the path that avoids pain is not necessarily the path to happiness.

Moving from pain to peace is not about avoiding fears but facing them. Moving from pain to peace is not about avoiding your own company but facing yourself. Being self-loving is about meeting yourself in the mirror and loving who you are and not what you look like, nor feeling that something is missing if you are standing alone.

"Him that I love I wish
to be free—
even from me."

—Anne Morrow Lindbergh

To Love and Be Loved
Is Life's Most Noble
Adventure

I was getting on a plane recently, and the fellow next to me asked what I did for a living. When I told him I was a writer, he asked what I was working on. I told him about this book and in particular this chapter on loving and being loved. "What a load of crap that is," said the man, who then turned back to his newspaper. And I laughed out loud, but his comment started me thinking.

For many of us, the idea of loving and being loved has a sissified air to it. That many of us, men in particular, tend to think that loving and being loved is not manly work only tends to confirm to me that any man who feels this way is a man who has his work cut out for him.

The reason for love is not reason.
Love is more than passion
and a person.
Love is intimacy with life.

To dare to live our lives with love is the kind of work that is a tale of knights and bravery and honor. Any of us hoping to move from pain to peace needs to know that this is not a fairy tale. At the same time, people who think that they can move from emotional pain to peace without opening their hearts are telling themselves a fairy tale.

Love requires us to love each other, not because we must, but because we can. To use Love as a guiding star to lead us out of pain doesn't mean the journey won't sometimes have pain. Falling in love is, after all, very different from landing. But the pain of love is nothing compared to the pain in a life without love.

"There is no remedy for love but to love more."

—Emerson

Make sure that at some point each day the needle on your Compass points to Love, otherwise no matter where you're heading, you're heading for pain.

Love Is in the Loving

Nothing so empowers us to move from pain to peace like love. Love fuels us to do what we never thought we could accomplish and to get past what we never thought we could surmount. And while the power of love needs a guardian at the gate—the role played by humility and honesty—with the guardian of these

Compass points in place, little is beyond our capacity.

The ability to access the power of love is a phenomenon not of knowing but of knowing through doing.

If there is any magic in the Compass for Healing it is the magic of Love. But love is no sleight of hand trick. Nor is it a reciprocal trade agreement. Love is the magic of what you get when you give. No one can move forward from pain to peace without the power of love. And being loving is the best way to play life forward.

Do not kiss your children so they will kiss you back but so they will kiss their children and their children's children.

"We can only learn to love
by loving."

—Iris Murdoch

A huge element in the power of love is the power of trust. You cannot hold the reins of love too tightly, for much of its power comes from simply giving it its head and letting it run. But this trust in love so nec-essary to access its power is yet another reason to make sure that the love is born in the soil of humility and honesty.

When you fall in love, you hand someone your heart. When you fall in love, you hand over your strength, your fears and your "please-don't-hurt-me," and you hand over so much you wonder if you have anything left to give anyone else, ever.

And when you have handed over all that, you fall on your knees and you thank God that you have been given the chance to give away what you would never, never allow anyone else to take. Gaining the power to move from pain to peace is as much about letting go as grasping. And there is nowhere that this truth is more true than in matters of the heart.

Anyone who has ever been in love has learned that there are lessons to be learned. Love, however, is much more than a classroom; it is an education in a class of its own.

Love's education is as poetic as it is absent of poetry, and brutal in its lessons. Lessons of the heart cut to the heart of all things.

*Love is a garden; as you sow so
shall you reap.
Plant pride; reap anger.
Plant humility; reap laughter.
Love is a blessing.
It is like the gentle dew that falls
on parched fields. Lovers are
quenched by each other.*

Love requires us to be honest with each other and to promise, first to ourselves, never to lie to each other out of the fear of being alone.

Love requires us to guard each other's solitude and the sanctity of solitude in a relationship.

Love requires us to love each other in sickness and in health, but it is not our work to heal the other or to do the other's work—and it is not our work because it is not work we can do.

Love requires us to remember that even when we can't heal one another, patience is a poultice, acceptance an analgesic and kindness its own cure.

Those who purport to tell you how to achieve happiness in life but can't be loving to others have lost their way to humility and honesty and to their own hearts. You can't move from pain to peace without love, and you can't get to love without humility and honesty. I know this may sound repetitive, but that is only because this is a matter that is so easily forgotten and so often sold as salvation even as it is empty of redemption.

"A new commandment
I give unto you, that you love
one another."

—Jesus

Love requires us to remember that we will often forget what we promise to remember. And remember, we all forget. And don't forget it.

Love requires us to remember that love opened our eyes, but to save our love we may have to close one eye, and to keep our love there may come times when we have to close both eyes.

While the path from pain to peace begins with

humbly and honestly accepting the pain you are feeling, and the power of love has much to do with the power of acceptance, this is not to be confused with accepting what's wrong as what's right, but as our shared vulnerability and it is from this vulnerability that we all begin.

---

*"A friend is one who
sees through you and still
enjoys the view."*

—Wilma Askinas

Love requires us to remember that love isn't about being right or being wrong, and anyone who is always right is usually wrong.

Love requires us to remember that when life's winds blow, what does not bend breaks.

Love requires us to be flexible. And the best way to stay flexible is to stretch. And the best stretch is to purposely make an effort to stretch each day away from our pain and toward peace.

Yoga means "union." There is a union between the pain and the peace in our lives. The work is in our determination to stretch from one to the other. And watch that we are stretching to the positive.

"Love knows hidden paths."

—German proverb

Love is a mystery. And its power is in its unfolding mystery. You cannot presume how love will impact your pain or move you to peace. Only that it will. And for each of us, this will occur in its own way.

Love requires us to treasure what we have in common, but to remain in love with one or many requires us to cherish our differences.

Love requires us to remember that love isn't about agreeing to get along but staying close with others when you're a long way away from agreeing.

> *"Let the dead have*
> *the immortality of fame,*
> *but the living the*
> *immortality of love."*
>
> —Rabindranath Tagore

Love is without boundaries. It knows no boundaries of power or time. It can arrive in a minute, last a lifetime, or lifetimes, or be gone in a whisper. It is this force that can blow away any pain and fill our day-to-day with unimagined peace.

While humility reminds us we are not in charge, and honesty reminds us to remember this, love is the embodiment of this.

Love requires us to remember that all of our lasting decisions are made in seasons of our minds that do not last.

Love requires us to remember that who we love is less important than who they might yet become—and us, too.

Love requires us to remember that love can be a

constant, but change is the only constant, and how we love will change, too, and to embrace love requires the courage to embrace change.

What is unchanging about love is the timeless truth that until you love yourself you can't love or be loved. So often when we are in pain over the issue of love, we look everywhere for what we think is missing and miss the self-embrace.

Love requires us to remember that the Golden Rule—not to do unto others what you would not do to yourself—is also the Golden Rule in love, and the Golden Rule, in love and lives, remains golden only if we also love ourselves. Otherwise we are prepared to treat others with the same disregard that we have for ourselves.

A huge part of our ability to love ourselves is the ability to embrace ourselves when we are less than our egos want us to be, and we don't have the honesty to be straight with ourselves about this. Again, until we visit Humility and Honesty, knowing Love is an impossibility. Once we accept the frailty of the human condition and love ourselves in our vulnerability then we can move from the pain of disappointment to making peace with being human.

Love requires us to remember that falling in love is very different from landing and being there to catch one another. Because we all fall. Because we all fail. Because we are all frail. Because we all need to be loved.

Love is not about agreeing with one another, or even agreeing with every aspect of our own personalities. It isn't about all of us looking at things the same way. It is about agreeing that we all have to look out for one another.

"Life has taught us
that love does not consist in
gazing at each other but
in looking outward together
in the same direction."

—Saint-Exupery

If we are in pain because our love seems to be lacking in intensity, then what we might take a look at are the two emotional strands, woven together, that and only when woven together, give love its tensile strength. It is only when passion and compassion are brought together and intertwined in our lives that the power of love has its healing capacity.

Love is made up of passion and compassion. Passion has built buildings and burned them down. Be as passionate about caring for others as you are passionate about your passions.

There is no more healing force than love. This is a truth known across time. This is a truth that cannot be taken away but is too often given away. Use this power that is at hand and in your heart and you will know, not only the wonders of healing, but also of being a healer to others.

READER/CUSTOMER CARE SURVEY

We care about your opinions! Please take a moment to fill out our online Reader Survey at **http://survey.hcibooks.com.**
As a **"THANK YOU"** you will receive a **VALUABLE INSTANT COUPON** towards future book purchases as well as a **SPECIAL GIFT** available only online! Or, you may mail this card back to us and we will send you a copy of our exciting catalog with your valuable coupon inside.

(PLEASE PRINT IN ALL CAPS)

First Name _____ MI. _____ Last Name _____

Address _____ City _____

State _____ Zip _____ Email _____

1. Gender
- ☐ Female   ☐ Male

2. Age
- ☐ 8 or younger
- ☐ 9-12   ☐ 13-16
- ☐ 17-20   ☐ 21-30
- ☐ 31+

3. Did you receive this book as a gift?
- ☐ Yes   ☐ No

4. Annual Household Income
- ☐ under $25,000
- ☐ $25,000 - $34,999
- ☐ $35,000 - $49,999
- ☐ $50,000 - $74,999
- ☐ over $75,000

5. What are the ages of the children living in your house?
- ☐ 0 - 14   ☐ 15+

6. Marital Status
- ☐ Single
- ☐ Married
- ☐ Divorced
- ☐ Widowed

7. How did you find out about the book?
(please choose one)
- ☐ Recommendation
- ☐ Store Display
- ☐ Online
- ☐ Catalog/Mailing
- ☐ Interview/Review

8. Where do you usually buy books?
(please choose one)
- ☐ Bookstore
- ☐ Online
- ☐ Book Club/Mail Order
- ☐ Price Club (Sam's Club, Costco's, etc.)
- ☐ Retail Store (Target, Wal-Mart, etc.)

9. What subject do you enjoy reading about the most?
(please choose one)
- ☐ Parenting/Family
- ☐ Relationships
- ☐ Recovery/Addictions
- ☐ Health/Nutrition
- ☐ Christianity
- ☐ Spirituality/Inspiration
- ☐ Business Self-help
- ☐ Women's Issues
- ☐ Sports

10. What attracts you most to a book?
(please choose one)
- ☐ Title
- ☐ Cover Design
- ☐ Author
- ☐ Content

TAPE IN MIDDLE; DO NOT STAPLE

BUSINESS REPLY MAIL
FIRST-CLASS MAIL PERMIT NO 45 DEERFIELD BEACH, FL

POSTAGE WILL BE PAID BY ADDRESSEE

Health Communications, Inc.
3201 SW 15th Street
Deerfield Beach FL 33442-9875

FOLD HERE

Comments

LOVE

Three Questions to Ask Yourself
When You Look at Love on Your Compass

1. Is what I am doing being loving to me?

2. Am I treating others as I would like to be treated?

3. Is my heart in what I am doing or saying?

LOVE

Some Loving Thoughts to Hold in Mind Under the Southern Star of Love

➤ Address someone you don't know as "my friend."

➤ Be passionate in what you choose as your passions.

➤ What is something, or someone, you lusted for and told yourself you loved?

➤ Give more than you get.

➤ Let go of more than you take.

➤ Release your hold on what is holding you back.

➤ Be forgiving of someone even when you remember why you're angry at them.

➤ Be prepared to chop wood to fuel your passion.

➤ It is your work to make amends. It is not your work to see that things are finally mended.

➤ Care when no one will reward you for it.

➤ Don't see others as others.

➤ Love is blind, but jealousy is blinding.

➤ The Talmud reminds us: "Kindness is the highest wisdom." Be cautious of those who want to be wiser than they are caring. Be cautious of those who confuse kindness with weakness.

➤ More than being giving—give a damn.

➤ Visit someone who is sick, and don't tell anyone.

➤ No good deed goes unpunished, but that's not an excuse to avoid good deeds.

➤ Good deeds are not a deal made with heaven. They are good for you, and that's good enough.

➤ Good deeds are love in the day-to-day. Make being loving a daily habit, and this habit will heal you day by day.

5

Faith:
The Western Star
on the Compass

> *"Without faith,*
> *nothing is possible.*
> *With faith, nothing is*
> *impossible."*
>
> —Mary McLeod Bethune

Belief says, "I believe I can." Faith says, "I can."

To have faith is to access a power greater than one's self. To have faith in others is to have faith that they can do the same. To have faith is to acknowledge what we can possess without making it a possession.

When we mix Humility, Honesty and Love with Faith, life is magic in the day-to-day and divine in eternity.

The good news is that if we humbly value who we are, are honest in our appraisal of the situation, bring passion and compassion to the effort and have faith—we can absolutely move from emotional pain to peace. The bad news is that without any one of these, we don't have a prayer.

Faith Serves Us in This World

Two hungry vultures are perched on a crag. The huge birds sit in silence watching the desert below them. The day drags on and on until finally, exasperated, one of the vultures turns to the other and says, "Forget about faith, let's go down there and kill something!"

The word "faith" is charged with personal and social implications. If we say someone is a person of faith, we tend to think that they believe in God. If we say someone is faithful, we tend to think that his wife can trust him. If we say that we take what someone says in good faith, we tend to think that it means we believe him or her. If we say someone is faithful to his or her effort, we tend to think that person will persevere against failure.

Sometimes faith is nothing more, and nothing less, than realizing that there are things at play in life that we simply can't see.

One night outside a little town, a guy was on the side of the road hitchhiking on a dark night in pouring rain. Time passed slowly and no cars went by. It was raining so hard he could hardly see a thing.

What he did see suddenly was a car moving slowly, approaching and appearing ghostlike in the rain. It slowly crept toward him and then stopped. Wanting a ride really badly, the guy jumped in the car and closed the door, only to realize that there was nobody behind the wheel. Then when the car slowly started moving, the guy was too terrified to think of jumping out and running.

When he saw that the car was slowly approaching a sharp curve, he was still too scared to jump out; he started to pray, begging for his life. He was sure the ghost car would go off the road and into the marsh and he would surely drown. Then just before the curve, a hand appeared through the driver's window and turned the steering wheel, guiding the car safely around the bend.

Still paralyzed with fear, the guy watched the hand suddenly reappear every time they reached a curve. Finally, scared to near death, he had all he could take and jumped out of the car and ran to the nearby town. Wet and in shock, he went into a bar and, voice quavering, ordered two shots of whiskey, then told everybody about his supernatural experience. A silence enveloped and everybody got goose bumps when they realized the guy was telling the truth and was not just some drunk.

About half an hour later two guys walked into the bar and one says to the other: "Look Bubba. There's that idiot who rode in our car when we was pushin' it in the rain."

Sometimes to experience the hand of faith in the day-to-day simply requires us to acknowledge that there are other hands in the universe, other than our own, that are on the helm.

While people tend to think of faith in religious terms, the Western star of Faith on the Compass for Healing is more about how we can move from pain to peace by having faith in one's self, one's children, one's work and one's vision for the future. Until we have calmed our egos, been honest and been loving, we cannot have the faith that we can move from pain to peace. Humility, Honesty and Love are the portals to having faith in our ability to heal, including our ability to heal our relationships with ourselves, with others and with the Divine.

Faith Can Get Us Through the Night

We are better people when we have faith in ourselves. We fulfill more of our own potential when we have faith that our children give us more than they can ever know. We are more for believing that the world we leave will be more for our being here, and whether we are more or less right about our notion of faith, the more is enough to get us through the night. And in each of our lives there is a darkest night—sometimes even at high noon.

Here is an apocryphal story that is well traveled and has helped a lot of people get through all kinds of emotional weather.

There was a little girl who was walking to school. The weather was foul, with wind and thunder and lightning, and because the little girl's mother was worried, she got into her car and drove along the route her child took to and from school.

What the mom saw was her little girl walking along smiling, jumping in and out of puddles. This was not the reaction to the storm that the mother had expected. The mother was even more surprised when, at each flash of lightning, the child stopped, looked up and smiled. As another and another flash followed quickly, the child repeated this pattern of turning to the heavens and flashing a grin.

When the mother's car drew up beside the girl, the mother lowered the window and asked her daughter, "What are you doing? Why do you keep stopping?"

And the child answered, "I am trying to look pretty because God keeps taking my picture."

In everyone's life some rain will fall. The question is how we will face our storms. The little girl in this story didn't know she was supposed to be afraid. She smiled in the face of danger and was sure heaven would smile back.

Life tends to do that. Life tends to smile on those who smile back. If you're looking for hope, look hopeful.

Faith Is Patience in Action

Faith is patience. Patience is power, waiting.
The hand that can hold itself back can do anything.

In the Occidental world it is generally thought that if you are not doing something, you're not doing something—and this is not a good thing.

Inaction and silence are far more valued in Eastern cultures than in the West. Faith is West on the new Compass, because when the sun goes down we live in a state of faith, divine or rational, that the night will give way to dawn. This fact does not require our doing anything but having patience and bearing witness, and often, little can make more of a healing impact on our life than being patient and paying attention.

Living in a state of faith means realizing how much we can achieve sometimes by taking our hands off the helm and letting nature and time—and the Divine if you are so inclined—to work its course.

"Patience moves mountains."

—Bedouin proverb

Having faith means giving our partners the time and space to show us they love us, giving our children the time and space to show us how great they can be, giving the people we work with the time and space to show us they can get the job done and giving ourselves the time to heal, mature and achieve all we might yet become—including becoming peaceful.

Faith is patience in the day-to-day. Too often when we run out of patience we're not crazy about what we run into. Leaving our patience, what we usually meet is our impatience.

I have often met my impatience and have found that it's like catching yourself in an unflattering angle in the mirror. You know it's you, but you wish it wasn't. All of us at some angles are definitely not angels, though even angels have their angles. Losing our faith we not only fall from grace but also we don't fall so gracefully, whether it's off a mountain or off the wagon.

Discovering who we are is an act of patience and faith. After all, we are, like anything else in the biosphere, a process—in our case, a person in process.

We are all emerging or, sometimes unfortunately, submerging. We are all just now coming into or wondering where we went. It doesn't matter how long it takes the partner in your life to get ready; the one most of us are waiting for is ourselves.

Faith and biochemists
remind us that, in our metaphysical
and physical makeup, any
aspect of us that is just now
arriving is just now leaving.
Over every finish line
in life are the words
"Begin here!"

For some of us, our peace is simply the part of us that is waiting to be born. Even if some of us feel we are born to wait. History often has less to do with great men or women and more to do with a man or woman who has arrived at a great moment at the right moment. You don't want to be late or arrive early to your life or at any decision in your personal or professional life. The success in anything we're pursuing might be the something beautiful waving its arms, desperately hoping we'll slow down so it can catch up.

"You can't push the river," says the Buddha, although many of us are feeling pushed to do just that. Faith is patience in the day-to-day. Patience is action in waiting.

*Opportunity dates people
of action but weds people
of patience.*

Faith Gives Birth to
the Best in Us

In one of Woody Allen's movies, he has a character who is asked what faith he is, and the character answers: "I was born of the Jewish faith but at fourteen converted to narcissism."

Faith in who we are is very different from narcissism, which is driven more by what we are afraid we are not, rather than a belief in the best in us.

Life is an act of gestation, a constant state of pregnancy. Patience is life's midwife. Screaming because you want to give birth right now doesn't right anything and doesn't hurry much in life along any sooner. If you doubt this, ask anyone who has been pregnant.

Like the movie business, we're all in development. We're all expecting. We're all becoming, even if we feel we don't look very becoming. Some of us will be fathers. Some of us will be moms. Some of us will be confused. All of us need to give birth to ourselves. We may not know who we will be, but we are all expecting, and like many who are expecting, we feel we are ready to give birth before we're ready. But we're not. Having faith that we will know when we're ready takes as much courage as having faith in what we do.

Giving birth is a struggle. Watching someone give

birth can also be a struggle. Wanting to do something when you can do nothing is one of life's great struggles. Some of us can't find the courage to do something. Some of us can't find the courage not to do something. Some of us can't find the courage to speak up. Some of us can't find the courage not to say something. We can be just as fearful of patience as action, of not doing as doing.

Many of the struggles that we observe in others we eventually come to see as our own. Sometimes in life it's a struggle just to realize how bound we are to one another and to have faith in the belief that we are all struggling to be born as the person we might yet be.

Before There Are No Butterflies

Once there was a man who found a cocoon of a butterfly and noticed a small opening where he assumed the butterfly would eventually emerge. The man waited and watched. Then to his dismay, he saw that the butterfly was having a very tough time squeezing out the hole.

The man decided he couldn't sit and watch this struggle, and so he took a small knife and made a small incision along the side of the hole so the butterfly would have an easier time of it. And the butterfly soon appeared.

What happened then was more concerning. The man noticed that the butterfly's wings were misshapen and couldn't fly. What the man didn't know was that the butterfly's normal struggle to make it through the small hole was designed by nature to squeeze the excess birth liquid from the butterfly's wings. And because the man "helped" and didn't wait for the natural process to take place, the butterfly would never fly.

Any of us who are in pain and hoping to gain peace need to remember that sometimes struggles are exactly what we need in our lives. If life allowed us to go through our lives without any obstacles, it would cripple us. We would not be as strong as what we could have been. And we could never fly.

What makes this story so touching is that the man is trying to do good. The man's efforts have the highest intentions, yet they are wrong. His good intentions are his failure. We can come to events in life with all of our integrity intact and be totally lacking in tact. In any moment what is just as important as our integrity is the integrity of the moment. Each moment has its drummer just as we do. Having faith in the integrity of a moment is no less important than honoring our own integrity. When we find our pace we can still be out of step with the universe.

It's tough to tell when we're in synch but out of step. Whether it's work, love or parenting, every process has its own timing and we must keep faith with that. Knowing the integrity of that process and sensing its timing takes faith's courage not to say something as much as the courage to speak up, the courage not to do something as much as the courage to jump in and make a proper muck of things.

The challenge for all of us is how to be in faith's cadence with one's self and at one with the planet's pace. There are micro and macro drummers, and sometimes we don't know how out of step we are until we have with pride and purpose marched ourselves into an emotional swamp.

Faith doesn't relieve us of right action at the right moment, but in a society that prides itself on what it can do, we might soon learn that our greatness is having faith in what we don't do.

Whether it's yourself, your patients, your children or the next generation, letting them struggle to be born, to learn to fly or to fly away may take the healing love of doing nothing. And in this faith in nonaction, we see our most loving acts.

Our fears for others are often our own fears, and to fight those fears we often feel we have to say something or do something even as faith in nonaction can be its own shield, its own sword, its own active force.

In the story of the butterfly there is testimony that life has its own pace; we need to discover that and to discover our own pace, and the sooner the better. And if it takes us a little longer than we hoped, have patience—with others and with ourselves.

People often ask how it is possible for there to be wars if God is in charge. I prefer not to see it as God's absence but God's patience—God's faith that we're learning. Hopefully we'll learn before we run out of butterflies.

"Our patience will achieve more than our force."

—Edmund Burke

What is a challenge in all of our lives, and the guiding light of the West on this Compass, is to learn the force of Faith. And to make that a force for good in your life.

Faith Is More Than a Fair-Weather Friend

One of the reasons Faith is the last point on the Compass is that Faith is where we can turn when we feel we can't turn anywhere else.

Faith isn't a fair-weather friend but a friend in all weather. Remember that the Compass is designed for people who are trying to get through all kinds of life storms. When your boat is in a safe harbor, you don't need a compass. When you want to move from pain to peace, the Compass for Healing can, with Faith, get you through any kind of storm in the world or your inner world.

Life can be an unexpected joy. Expect that. Faith sees around corners.

"Sometimes you have to jump off the cliff and build your wings on the way down."

—Ray Bradbury

Reason can take us only so far in life. When we get to the end of reason's road, life necessitates a leap of faith. In that leap of faith, spirituality is a cosmic seat belt.

Moving from pain to peace is not a mystery. It is only a mystery to those who see it as a solution outside of themselves rather than having the faith that they are the source of their own healing.

It betters the odds on healing when the patient has faith in the doctor and the doctor has faith in the patient. And especially when the patient and doctor are one in the same. Faith is basically a belief that goes beyond the evidence that supports it and yet it can support us.

"Faith is an oasis in the heart which will never be reached by the caravan of thinking."

—Kahlil Gibran

In a religious context, belief in a divine being that cannot be scientifically identified or proven is called "faith." In a similar way, beliefs in your own worth and significance are also manifestations of faith. You may not have the evidence to prove any of the assumptions about your talent, and worth, and power to heal, but there is power in your positive faith. Clearly, every important figure across history has demonstrated a kind of faith in his or her life by living a full and visionary life with no guarantees of success. Celebrate your uniqueness and unlimited potential. No one else has your thoughts, ideas or ways of doing things. Each of us has unlimited talents, potentials and possibilities. And each of us needs to have faith in that.

---

*"It is difficult to make
a man miserable while he feels
he is worthy of himself and
claims kindred to the great
God who made him."*

—Abraham Lincoln

Finding faith is itself an act of faith. A lot of us feel we don't even know where to begin looking. But if we acknowledge that we are a reflection of something more than ourselves, if we are honest about wanting to access something greater than ourselves and if we are compelled by love rather than power, we will find that we have the power of faith, and what we feel we can't grasp, we will find is at our fingertips.

"Intuition will tell the thinking
mind where to look next."

—Dr. Jonas Salk

Faith is the intuitive knowledge that we have the power within us to move from pain to peace—and a reminder that this inner capacity cannot be taken from us but is too often given away.

Inspire Your Faith in You

Comparing ourselves to others never has positive benefits. The Buddha put it best when he said, "If you do not get it from yourself, where will you go for it?" Knowing this truth can transform your life.

At some point you have either inspired or deflated others. That power is within you. You know that. That leaves only you with the decision of whether you are going to inspire to the dark side or to the light. And if you can impact others, why not radiate faith and confidence in your power and your purpose in the world?

This capability and responsibility lies squarely on your shoulders. The capability and responsibility to nurture, develop and have faith in people is in your power.

If we don't exercise faith in ourselves, we will most likely meet our expectations. And if we don't exercise faith in others, counting on our faith in them, they will also most likely meet our expectations.

> Faith straps us to the cosmos and reminds us that we are connected to something much greater than us— much greater than this moment we are operating in. Shared faith reminds us that we are all neighbors in time, and in this neighborhood none of us are alone.

Most parents are aware that teachers' expectations about children often become self-fulfilling prophecies. If a teacher believes a child is slow, the child will also come to believe that and will indeed learn slowly. The child who strikes a teacher as bright also picks up on that expectation and will work to confirm that expectation. This finding has been validated so many times and in such varied settings that it's no longer even debated. Self-fulfilling prophecies, it turns out, are just as prevalent in the hospital room as they are in the classroom. If a health-care professional is convinced that the people with medical care can get better, this belief might not make them better, but it certainly gives them a better chance.

Having faith in who we are and who we can become, and in our ability to move from pain to peace, is more than wishful thinking. Faith in what we are thinking dramatically heightens the odds that our wishes can come true. And if you question the wisdom of faith, perhaps you might also want to think about the wisdom of enlightened despair.

> *"Every tomorrow has*
> *two handles; we can take hold*
> *of it with the handle of anxiety*
> *or the handle of faith."*
>
> —Henry Ward Beecher

The intellectual whose wit gives him- or herself no peace has given away the larger part of wisdom. Those who use their minds as a reason not to have faith have reasoned themselves into existential defeat, or what I call "sadness that went to college." Life presses in on all of us regardless of our IQ. Real wisdom isn't about knowing more but living better. Having faith that moving from pain to peace is worth the effort is a no-brainer that can be especially challenging to those blessed with brains.

Having Faith in Others
Can Change Their Lives, Too

What isn't said between people is also heard. Indifferent and noncommittal treatment communicates low expectations and leads to performances that meet those expectations. What we think we or others can or can't do has power. Faith is not an indifferent force. Faith, in ourselves and others, is what can make all the difference. What is the way someone signaled you when you were a child or in your adult life that showed they didn't have faith in you? How did that feel?

Faith is a healing tool. And healing emotionally can simply mean moving from however someone else feels about you to having faith in how you feel about yourself. When we experience this in our lives, we come to realize how much our having faith in someone can be a positive for them in their healing so they can reidentify themselves and grow to have the self-respect they always needed but with which they were never nurtured. Faith, like Humility,

Honesty and Love, not only has power for us; it also has a contagious power that can be lent to others.

Phillip and Louise

When Phillip was growing up he was physically abused by his father. Louise grew up with a mother who wanted more to be one of the girls than a mother. When Phillip and Louise met, they were both looking and hoping for someone in whom they could have faith. They talked about this early in their relationship and made a vow that regardless of their attractions to each other that they would also have faith in each other. In doing so they become cross-contagiously hopeful of the best in each other, and their relationship believes in that expectation. We often don't realize the power of people having faith in each other until we witness couples, parents and children, or working relationships of any nature that operate without faith in each other and soon tumble to meet that expectation.

◆ ◆ ◆

David and Josh

David comes from a blue-collar background. He was the first person in his family who not only graduated from college but also from high school. David was bright, motivated and competitive. Being a good student was his rocket ship out of his family's economic situation. David's son Josh is also very bright but more interested in athletics than what college he will attend. Because David has nothing in his own experience like this, he tries to motivate Josh by being a "pain in the ass." "Didya, didya, didya" becomes David's litany to Josh. Then one day, someone tells David about the Compass and the Western star of Faith, and David tries a different tack with his son than the repeated pattern that was bringing neither of them any peace. "Josh," says David, "my time with you is too fleeting to be the resident pain. So here's the story. I think you're bright and talented and you can do whatever you want to achieve. And I have all the faith in the world in you and will lend you any support I can. But it has to be you that does it. And if you don't, those results will be yours as well. Because of my circumstances it was easier for me, I was driven by need. You need to be driven by character." And then David stepped back and let Josh step forward. Josh did, and Josh loves his father for his Faith.

Research shows that people in any relationship do best not when they most accurately observe the least in each other but rather when they observe the best.

The password for lasting love and best work performance is not to avoid a favorable impression but to have the faith to sustain it. This doesn't mean we do best when we lie to each other but simply when we choose to see the best and have faith that if we look for the best in people we will more often than not find it.

Faith reminds us that most of us find what we're looking for in life. To be self- and other-healing requires us to be cautious of what our faith envisions.

People without positive faith who call themselves realists may be well-informed about information that can influence outcome and the difficulties ahead, but people who have positive faith in their ability to move from pain to peace far more often realize their goals and feel better about their outcomes.

A person of faith reminds me of the boy who sees a room filled with manure and grabs a shovel believing there must be a pony buried somewhere.

A person of faith is one who is convinced that every time a door shuts another one opens.

FAITH

Three Questions to Ask Yourself When You Look at Faith on Your Compass

1. At this very moment, am I being faithful to who I am?

2. Do I have faith that I can get past the things that caused me pain in the past?

3. Do I have faith that no matter what happens to me or what others say to me, if I am humble, honest and loving that I am okay with me because there is nothing more I can do?

FAITH

Some Thoughts to Hold Faith with and That Will Hug You Under the Western Star of Faith

➤ Do something only on faith, and if doesn't work out, do it again.

➤ Tell a kid you believe in him or her. Tell them again. Tell yourself the same thing.

➤ Have patience with someone you love. Remind yourself that you don't just love them in the moment but across time, and that across time they will need to have the same patience with you.

➤ Prayer is not room service. God is not a cosmic bellhop.

➤ God does make house calls if you invite God into your home.

➤ Admit to yourself when you talk about having faith in God but lose your patience with people. Have patience with yourself on this issue.

➤ Think about something that happened after you had done everything you could, and nothing happened, and you felt nothing would. Remember this.

➤ Remember that God isn't done with you yet, and you are a work of art but a work in progress. Others are, too.

➤ Faith's road sign reads: When you are in a hurry, go slowly.

➤ Hope for the best; make peace with the rest.

➤ The best way to make it through the day is to remember you only have to make it through one day at a time. Every day.

➤ Do everything you can to make something you really want to happen, happen. Do it humbly, honestly, passionately and compassionately, and then turn away and be patient. And have faith for a little longer yet.

➤ Faith is a reminder that often the most important thing we can do in life is what we choose not to do. And sometimes there is nothing more important we can do than to let go and let God.

➤ Faith reminds us that we are a reflection of divine love, and as a result, God would love for us to have a great time while we are here.

➤ Pray less "please" and more "thank you."

➤ If you're waiting patiently to hear from God, remember God may be waiting to hear from you.

➤ Life can be an unexpected joy. Expect that. Remember: faith sees around corners.

6

How the Compass
Can Help You
Get Past Roadblocks
and Detours

In all of our lives there are roadblocks and detours. Some of these are roadblocks and detours we have built out of pride, dishonesty, absent love and lack of faith. Some of these are the simple results of events outside ourselves. The irony, however, is that some of these actually serve us. Some of them take us, begrudgingly, down veering paths to better places than we could have imagined. Sometimes the disappointment we feel about where our path is taking us isn't disappointment in where we're heading but because the path is outside our egos' narrow intention. Sometimes in life, we get dragged kicking and screaming to a better place.

The path from pain to peace does not follow the straight and narrow, and there are many paths—one for each of us at each of the moments in our lives. Your path will be yours alone. That doesn't mean you will be alone, but that your path is yours alone. So if the first source of your pain is the concern that you feel detoured or roadblocked because your path doesn't look like the path of others, it shouldn't. Your path in life is as individual as you, and if you try to make someone else's path yours, that is one of the surest paths to pain.

All of us have received what I call "going-away presents" from our parents and family: attitudes, perspectives and veils on the world that were given to us, sometimes unintentionally and unknowingly, by those who came before us and who were lost in some way on their own journey from things in their own past.

> On the highway of life, watch for illusion to cross your path; brake for the truth.

These white elephants only have value when we see them as the roadblocks and detours they are and not for the insurmountable barriers they may appear as.

The cartoonist Jules Feiffer once wrote, "I grew up to have my father's looks—my father's speech patterns—my father's posture—my father's opinions—

and my mother's contempt for my father."

Too often we take the roadblocks and detours given to us by the past and use them to make our own stumbling blocks in the present. We might call this "living life in the past lane." Most of us aren't conscious of how much the past influences us. We are simply trying to do the day-to-day work of getting through the day. Old mistakes are often used to prop up new mistakes until we discover we have built a wall in front of us that we never remember deciding to build and have no idea how to take down. Trying to reassemble our lives generally feels like way too much work when we may be in pain but are exhausted and are thereby allowing the past to exhaust our future.

---

*"Nothing weighs heavier
on the lives of children than the
unlived lives of parents."*
—Carl Jung

When you use the Compass you will see these roadblocks and detours in your life. The Compass will help you take down what others have constructed, and help you keep from turning your building blocks into stumbling blocks. This may seem like a huge task, but it isn't. It's just how you decide to look at things. A refusal to open your eyes takes much more work than a willingness to open them. The journey from pain to peace is not without stumbling blocks and detours because your life isn't. The journey from pain to peace is a journey you can not only take but also take responsibility for and make. The journey from pain to peace is already happening. You are already in process because you are not a sum but a process.

Finding our way from pain to peace is not simple. But neither is the path to finding our way hidden. Rather, most of us have had our eyes shut some of the time, or have been trained to see through the veil of eyes half-shut, or are blinded to the awareness that the obvious is often camouflaged by its obviousness.

It is not the philosopher's job to make simple

things difficult but to make difficult things simple. While all of us have our work cut out for us, it is also work we are cut out to do, can do and will feel better for doing. And nothing feels better than feeling better.

If you are laughing at the idea that you can actually get past the roadblocks and detours that have stymied you across time, that is a good sign. Just as laughing is sometimes the best way to cry, humor is often the best way to summon our courage in the same way that courage is often only fears that have said their prayers.

The average child will fall three hundred times before he or she learns to walk. So, unless you crawled to the store to buy this book, or crawled from your bed to the computer to order it, you clearly have the courage and will within your personal history—as testified in your ability to walk—to do the work at hand, get past the roadblocks and detours and get on with the journey from pain to peace.

Getting Past the Detour
of Not Taking an Honest Look

Nothing is more of a witness to the heroism of daily living than having the courage to take an honest look at our lives. The ability to step back from our own canvas allows us to see that we are a work of art, but also a work in process.

If we want to honor the getting to peace process in our lives, we have to begin by giving honest witness to what brought us pain. We have to accept that, for each of us, our experiences of pain are individual and cannot be measured against someone else's. So if someone you know has had the same thing happen to them that happened to you but seems to be in a better place, good for them. That doesn't mean you are any less, only that you are 100 percent you—on your path. None of us feel hot water or life's chill in the same way, or have the same feelings when falling in love even if we know what it is to fall in love. We may have ways to describe the various sensations to one another, but when we say the rose is red, all we're agreeing on is that the color that looks red to us is what someone else also chooses to call "red." Our individual experiences of pain and peace are as personal as we are different persons.

Not only do we experience pain as individuals, but for each of us the pain we experience is hyper-personal. Who has the right to measure the pain that comes from experiencing a childhood divorce versus the pain of child abuse? Who has the right to measure what it is like to have an alcoholic parent against what it means to be an alcoholic? Who has the right to measure what it means to be poverty stricken as a child against a middle-aged poverty of the spirit? Who can measure the pain of feeling alone in the night as a child against the painful fear of dying alone? Who has the right to stand in judgment about feeling fat as a kid against growing fat and feeling ignored by a spouse? Who can measure the difference between being told you were stupid as a child and growing old and being treated as inane by your children? Who can total and compare the sum of pain between losing a parent as a child, losing a child or losing a spouse— the love of your life? Who can, and who wants to?

The number of ways we can experience pain and

the nature of the pain we might have experienced are as varied as our ability to be inhumane and indifferent to each other and to ourselves. But no matter the face your pain wears, the Compass for Healing reminders can help you not simply paste on a happy face but help you face the facts and find not just a way but a peaceful way to find peace.

Moving from pain to peace is work but needs to be seen as a labor of self-love—a love perhaps too long self-denied.

---

*We don't have to be
perfect to be loved, and we
won't get perfect love.*

Getting Past the Roadblock
of Fear of Beginning

If the prospect of attempting to move from pain to peace frightens you in some way, that's okay. That only means you understand and respect the nature of the task you are undertaking, and in respecting the challenge you are respecting yourself—certainly the first step in the journey.

All of our strengths were born as fears.

The truth is that we all have fears, and while fear is often the pain behind the wound, it is also often the pain before the wound. This leads us to perhaps the most relevant question to doing the work at hand: in our day-to-day lives, do we serve our fears, and can we instead find a way for them to serve us?

A lot of us say we want to move from pain to peace but are afraid to begin the journey. Many of us mask this fear with a lot of other names, from being too late in life to not having the time to really focus on change.

The Compass for Healing, however, operates on the principle that no one has ever found their way who has not felt lost. So being afraid that you feel lost or that you have fears doesn't mean you can't move from pain to peace. Rather, such fear is the human condition from which all progress can be made.

If you acknowledge you have a fear, then that is the place to begin. You start with what's bothering you.

Many people are fearful of failure because they have taken so long to commit to doing something about the pain in their lives. Many people are even embarrassed to ask themselves, "Why has it taken me so long to really commit to do something about the pain in my life?"

Feeling fearful of beginning already means you are not as alone as you might feel. Taking a long time to commit to doing something about your pain doesn't make you foolish. It only means you're in pain, feeling what most of us, at one time or another, have felt.

We all know when we're in pain, but many of us make ourselves so busy so as to not face the pain. Too often we hide what we're not dealing with by being busy doing so much.

For some of us, doing something about our pain begins with simply recognizing a pain that has been a part of life for so long that it is a white noise whose silence is deafening. The comedian Buddy Hackett said, "I didn't know what heartburn was until I went into the army, and for the first time in my life there was this strange burning sensation that was no longer in my chest." For many of us, our decision to seek an alternative to our pain doesn't occur until the moment we realize what we've been missing. If you feel there is something profoundly missing in your life, this is a profound awareness from which anything is possible.

We are like people with lanterns
going in search of a light.

Beating yourself up about not doing something about your pain will not put you in less pain. Indeed, it may be because of your pain that you're inclined to beat yourself up—or because someone else or the randomness of life beat you up emotionally, intellectually or physically, and it's too tough to get over it, face it or feel righteously angry that it happened. This is not a flaw in your life but a fact that makes you even more deserving of an arm around your shoulder rather than an accusing finger poking you in the chest.

Almost none of us put ourselves in pain purposely, but to get out of pain takes great purpose and, as it happens, can borrow on the strength you have developed in simply surviving your pain.

The pain is in you. So is the peace. You are the bridge to both, and you have the strength to span both. Don't worry about all the times you didn't cross that bridge. Now's the time to get over it.

Our fears only have the strength we give them.

Getting Past the Roadblock of "But How Long Will It Take Me to Find Peace?"

There is no schedule for finding peace. When people ask me how long it will take until they find peace, I tell them, "The honest answer is, I don't know." I do know that any of us can find our way in a moment and lose our way at any moment. I also know that how long it takes to find peace is less important than if you're on the way because that means you are already leaving pain behind, and feeling better begins by *wanting* to feel better, *now*.

Time is an orchard;
every moment is ripe
with opportunity.

While we don't always find what we're looking for, it's a pretty good bet that being hopeful is the best way to go looking for hope.

There was a farmer who had many troubles, so each night before he entered his home he touched a tree by the front door. When he left in the morning he again touched the tree. When asked why he did this, the man answered, "I touch the tree at night and hang up my troubles before I enter the house, and I am hopeful that there will be fewer problems in the morning. Sure enough, as long as I hang up my troubles with hope, when I leave in the morning I generally discover I have less."

The truth does not go into hiding because we shut our eyes. Peace is a constant. It is we who are fickle and come and go with our emotional tides. We can influence peace's arrival, and we can certainly hasten its departure. But whether we are hoping to lure peace or pursue it, acknowledge that a moment's peace is a blessing in life and worthy of the pursuit. A concern for how long it will take to find peace is hardly a reason to derail our intentions.

Getting Past the
Roadblock of Denial

The contagion of denial is highly infectious. Never underestimate the power of denial because it has, at one time or another, held its power over and been a cause of demonic power in all of us. The power of denial doesn't mean simply how much we can deny but refers to the volcanic power that eventually erupts in our lives when we live a life of denial.

The problem with denial, to quote Henry Kissinger, is that, "A problem avoided is a crisis invented."

Knowing we are in pain is different from knowing we want to do something about it. And knowing we want to do something about our pain is very different from knowing what to do.

On reflection, it becomes apparent that few of us are lacking for information; most of us instead are lacking the character to act on the information at hand.

The emotional pain in our lives is an accumulation of people, events, actions and words spoken and not spoken over a lifetime. The causes of our pain could have happened to us in a single night or because of how we were forced to go to bed night after night for a lifetime. Our pain is something that has been at work for a long time; at some points, sadly, we may ourselves have been twisting and contorting events to set the stage for our sad play to play out. Even if we feel, perhaps very deservedly, that we are victims finally learning to feel different about ourselves, as with all learning this also takes a little time.

It is not "now or never," but now is never again.

Now is the time to take that moment and take yourself to a better place. You deserve it. You certainly don't deserve any less. No one does. People who live in pain are contagious and eventually put others in pain. People who live in peace are also contagious and eventually bring others to peace. Healing yourself will not only heal you, but also is the most grassroots way to help heal the world.

If there was a mission statement to the Compass's message it would be as follows: No more victims and not another day letting the negative forces affecting you convince you to continue holding yourself as a victim in any aspect of your life with yourself or with anyone else.

Too many of us are caught in pain, and it is too sad. But sadder is the way too many of us beat ourselves up because of the bad things that happened to us.

Too many of us, especially when we were children, interpret the bad stuff happening to us as a lesson that we did something bad. Bad stuff does happen, too often, to good people and too often to innocent people. And this is something too important for us to forget.

None of us wears a big S under our clothing for Superman or Superwoman. All of us do wear a big V for vulnerable. This is our shared humanity and our shared opportunity for heroism.

When we are dealing with pain that has a long history, it is hard to get past what we know as our norm. To help in dealing with this norm, consider this perspective on an old story:

God told Noah to build an ark because a flood was coming, Noah was also commanded to build a window in the ark so that he and his family could tell when the rain had stopped and when the sun had come out—when to come out of the ark.

Painful floods affect all of our lives. These can be floods of alcohol, drugs, food, childhood abuse, an abusive mate, an abusive government or simply the abuse of poverty.

What most of us usually do to avoid any of these floods—and all the others—is build an ark, but not necessarily an ark of wood. For most of us the ark we build and run to to survive the painful stuff in life is a habit, a denial, a purposeful ignoring, a reaction pattern of some kind, and for some a neurotic hiding place or worse. For some of us the ark might be to eat too much, cry too much, spend too much or make as much money as possible and bankrupt our spirits. In the face of the pain raining on us and in the moment of it, we might actually need these survival habits because in some sense they give us shelter from the storm—or seem to—at the time.

But while the ark of any survival pattern may momentarily help us survive the bad times, the higher calling is to learn that when the raining pain has passed, it is time for us to come out of the ark of these habits and not to live in the pain of the past, but to come out of the habits the pain built.

One of the early psychologists said, "I can't grow a beard because my father had one." Because we had nothing to eat as kids doesn't sentence us by reaction pattern to the pain of being fat adults. Because we were abused as kids doesn't mean we have to strike back at the next generation. Because we were bullied doesn't mean we need to bully others to know we are no longer victims. Because our parents were alcoholics doesn't mean we have to live our lives as dry drunks. Because our parents divorced doesn't mean we have to lock our hearts so we're not hurt by a partner we hope will love us and have our solution be a self-fulfilling prophecy of loneliness.

While it sometimes takes time, sometimes a lot of time, for the rain/pain to pass, more often what takes time is bearing witness that the rain has stopped; and the courage and will it takes us to step out of the ark and learn to walk in healthy peace on the good land we have been given; and to witness God's promise in the rainbow overhead that this storm will not return; and at the end of the day to find that our peace is not over the horizon, but within us.

Getting Over the Destructive Detour of Perfection, Embarrassment and Shame

---

"The pursuit of perfection is an impediment to improvement."

—George Will

Depression is the number-one mental illness in North America, and the source of most depression is stress. The source of most stress comes from trying to be in control of things that are out of our control. The pursuit of perfection is not the pursuit of excellence but the pursuit of control.

Pain does not reflect the lack of perfection; the pursuit of perfection is its own pain. If you doubt this, ask any honest person whose life is centered on perfection.

There is no basis for shame or embarrassment in feeling pain. There is shame on those who have done things to you that made you feel that way and whose judgment you accepted. There is shame on those who for their own reasons would want to hoist that shame on you. There is only heroism on you for wanting to leave your pain behind, and only those who have made this effort of bravery under the fire of social pressure can truly honor the private courage of others.

The insidiousness of past pain is that it can snake in and constrict our future and make us feel guilty. When we feel ashamed for being in pain, we are still empowering the past—often our victim past—rather than the future.

We all have fears from the past. Fears are of necessity born in the past, even as they live in the present and bring dread of the future—unless they are addressed.

People in pain are not necessarily people who are wrong. More often they are people who have been wronged. Even so, healing is not about pointing fingers at others; it is about remembering to point yourself in the right direction.

The feeding ground for the detours of shame and embarrassment is the fear of isolation. But in experiencing pain we are alone together with everyone else.

We all have emotions. We all have emotional pain in our lives. But for each of us our experiences of pain is as individual as we are. If you want to know why you feel so alone in your pain, it is not because only you are in pain, but because your experience of the pain is individuated.

Still, we often can't believe, or don't want to believe, that others are feeling the pain we are feeling. We think that if we're the only one experiencing the pain, then this experience makes us an individual.

However, it doesn't serve us to look for self-worth in our individual experiences of pain or self-pity. Rather, in working with the Compass we come to see that facing our fears and pain is what makes us individuals and allows us to view ourselves as heroic.

Outside a bar in Cabo San Lucas, I once saw a sign that read "Admission limited to members and non-members only." The same is true with emotional pain. It is humanity's shared experience and in many ways our shared humanity.

Some of us have been detoured from finding our way to peace because we have felt guilty for being in emotional pain. It's hard to look at a beautiful newborn and imagine that even this innocent, glorious being is going to have his or her share of grief.

If you think that life is a picnic, here are the ants: There is not a single person alive who does not have emotional problems, even if they are only imaginary problems. The problems in life that we don't want to face still have every intention of being in our faces.

Just because we decide to
shut our eyes does not mean the
world goes into hiding.

Into each of our lives some life creeps, sometimes in the form of a creep and sometimes creepy things.

The Buddha said life is suffering, and the source of all suffering is attachment. So as long as we're attached to being alive, feeling alive, to being with others—and even attached to attaining Nirvana—we are going to experience some emotional pain.

Of course, you can resign yourself to simply being in emotional pain and spend your life trying to suffer with dignity, or complaining, but that's a rough and boring—let alone lonely—road, unless you enroll in the various "wound societies" whose byword is "life is unfair and look what happened to me."

Or you can do something about the emotional pain that is part of living and get on with your life and make a commitment to take responsibility for moving from pain to peace.

Your attitude is self-contagious. You dramatically influence whether you are raising yourself up or putting yourself down.

My friend's eighty-five-year-old aunt Edith was generally happy no matter how much life turned her life upside down. She was born a princess, suffered the Holocaust, lost much and still held to what was sacred, cherished and joyous.

When I asked her the secret, she said, "A long time ago it struck me that no matter what happened I could be happy or sad, and I just decided to be happy."

"That just sounds like common sense," I told Aunt Edith.

And she replied, "I don't know why they call it common sense. It's not that common."

Attitude is altitude.
Life rains on all of us.
A good attitude will allow you
to witness that tears falling
from heaven are also watering
your garden . . . and can
cause you to bloom.

If you want to find your way to doing something more than throw in the towel, if you want to find your way to doing something more than pointing fingers, if you want to find your way to doing more than attending your own pity party, if you want to find your way embracing the joy that is also part of life no less than the pain, get a Compass. The best is yet to come. The best in you is waiting.

Getting Past Other People as Stumbling Blocks

People who cross your path in life can be both a pain and a salvation. Some are both. Sometimes we are both to ourselves.

Most of us in this wide world are caught up in our own little world. People generally don't do things to us; they do things for them.

As far as emotionally hurting others, we can be both innocent and guilty. Too many of us don't witness how often the havoc of trying to survive our own lives can negatively impact the lives of others.

One example is the young girl whose mother never played the role of mother, who then over-mothers her own children, suffocating them with the love she never received.

A classic and yet even sadder example is people who have been abused as children and survived by closing off their ability to feel. They may later fall in love, and actually want to be loved, but can't allow others in because of a fear of being hurt. The absent parent from the past becomes the present emotional roadblock to peace.

---

*"Life is 10 percent
what you make of it and
90 percent how you take it."*

—Irving Berlin

Still others are sadly more than trapped. Their idea of nurturing themselves is to nurture pain in others. The Compass is a weapon that can help you fend off the innocent and/or purposeful destructive habits of others by sharpening positive habits of your own. The Compass can also serve as a shield so you don't let the opinions of others confuse your opinion of yourself.

Humility leads us to self-esteem and shields us from needing to be the trained seal for whoever will throw us a fish. Honesty reminds us not to take onto ourselves the emotional wreckage that doesn't belong to us and that someone else is handing us. Love, and self love, reminds us that we can disagree with others and love them for their failings, without needing to get angry to say "no." Faith reminds us that when others let us down, we don't have to lose faith in who we are or might yet become.

Yes, there will always be people in the world who confuse kindness with weakness. And, yes, there will always be people, perhaps people like you, who are too gentle to live among wolves. To that end, as you read on you will see how to use the Compass for Healing as both emotional armor and a built-in directional finder.

7

How the Compass
Can Serve as
Emotional Armor
and a Built-in
Directional Finder

The Compass
as Emotional Armor

Perhaps nothing is more common and makes us more vulnerable than confusing how we feel with who we are. Moving from pain to peace requires us to distinguish the difference, which isn't hard to see, but does require that we take the time to look at the Compass. The Compass allows you to discern between the two and affords you emotional armor so that even when the world bombards you with its emotional stuff you can sort out "my stuff" from "the world's stuff."

Under the North star of Humility, we can see that ego is a drama queen. Our egos like to drag us into being hurt, taking offense, being victorious and feeling retributive when the ego feels it isn't getting enough attention or the kind of attention it has in mind. But we don't have to confuse how we're feeling with who we are.

The Taoist masters teach: "To take offense is to give offense." Our best defense may be a refusal to let our egos take offense.

Humility and Honesty are character armor. They require us to return to others what isn't ours. This doesn't mean giving others a dose of the discontent they may have given us. It does mean we simply don't have to accept what isn't our stuff. Humility on the Compass reminds us that we already have enough of our own stuff to work through, and Honesty reminds us that we can't do anyone else's work—just as they can't do ours.

Often the best emotional armor in life is simply to wear more Teflon and less Velcro. One of the best armor suits we can wear in our emotional lives is to simply not let other people's stuff stick to us and to let our inflated self-importance slip away.

The Southern star of Love is the armor of self-love. The Western star of Faith is the armor of having faith in ourselves. If you dismiss either of these armors you are giving away some of life's most protective forces.

An important distinction should be made between the Compass's emotional armor and traditional armor. Unlike traditional armor, the Compass's emotional armor . . .

> doesn't weigh on us; rather, it lessens our burden;
> doesn't need to be put on or taken off; it is the
> blessing of who you are;
> doesn't tarnish in bad emotional weather; it
> grows stronger the more emotional weather
> it endures.

The Compass is emotional armor, but it doesn't protect you from having emotions. Rather, it allows you to put your emotions to good purpose, to teach you, to serve you, to help you feel better about who you are. The success of the Compass is not in rising above feeling but feeling better by being your best you.

The Compass as Built-in Directional Finder

We are all born with a built-in directional finder to what is of value. Often we can sense this more than we can see it. Most of us forget that we have a built-in directional finder until we feel lost. But that we feel lost means we can tell the difference between where we should be and where we are, even if we can only sense this from our discomfort.

The good news is that our built-in directional finder to the best in us has infinite patience and is waiting for us to show up. Once we do, the real show begins.

Finding our way often means
we simply have to explore
where we're getting lost.

The Compass's four stars of Humility, Honesty, Love and Faith are a cosmic night-light. These stars burn bright within us, and by turning to them we can find our way on the darkest nights.

Anytime you locate yourself in relationship to these four stars you will not be lost. You may be scared. You may find the path new. But you will not be lost. And you will absolutely be on the path to peace.

If any one of these Compass points falls from your veil of orientation, you will be misdirecting yourself and instead using old habits that caused you to become lost over and over again. These old habits constantly emotionally argue for your attention by touting the familiar but negative over the healthy but new.

What we think is happening to us isn't always what's happening. Sometimes we feed ourselves wrong information to support what we want to believe and not because of what is actually happening to us. The Compass makes you stop and take a reading on reality.

On the instrument panels of Israeli military jets there are two altimeters. The reason for having two is that aeronautic engineers in Israel discovered that even the best pilots going at supersonic speeds can get turned upside down in the dark and refuse to accept they are heading for a crash when they believe they are heading to the stars. Understanding this, the engineers now put two altimeters in the plane so the pilots cannot convince themselves that both altimeters are in error. The Compass for Healing is unfailing. It is a built-in directional finder if we will exercise the courage and will to look at the directional markers of Humility, Honesty, Love and Faith and how they are playing in our lives. When our lives pick up speed, when we are convinced we are heading to the stars, taking a look at the Compass remains a good idea.

This is also true when the world around us is giving us its opinion of the right thing to do. Taking a look at the Compass, your inner directional finder, hereto remains a good idea. The truth doesn't need a majority to be the truth.

Sailors didn't sail over the edge of the world because mapmakers thought the world was flat.

The truth is that most of us decide what lies we want to believe, and we need that because when we're in emotional pain, we all tell ourselves lies to get us through the night.

Who among us has not told ourselves a lie? *He loves me even if he's hurting me. My mother couldn't help what she did. I will stop being victimized by my anger. I really love this job. I will lose weight tomorrow. I can stop drinking tomorrow. My father will get well.* We do this not because we believe it, but because we need to believe it, and that doesn't make us "bad." But it also doesn't necessarily bring us the results we had in mind. Getting straight with our egos, our honesty, our need for love and our faith/ lack of faith and need for faith can help us head in the right direction.

The Compass is a built-in directional finder so we can find our way to the bright new day that is dawning if we will have the will and courage to open our eyes.

The Compass is a built-in directional finder that will function as a friend and teacher. With the Compass you will find a guide to the peace in making good company of yourself.

Conclusion

How the Compass Can Help Us by Helping Others

It has taken me a lifetime to learn and nine years to write this book. I have written this book as a gift to all of us, and to remind us of this gift that is in all of us. The Compass is a shared gift about what matters and what has been learned across time, and whose single purpose is to be an ally to people across time. The sacred truth of the Compass is that it is a gift only when it is opened and more of a gift when it is passed along.

The Compass for Healing can be taught to anyone. It can be used to protect and help your children, and to help friends, and coworkers, and anyone with whom you will share the kindness of caring. It can be and should be used because all of us in life are in it together, and because we need to be a Compass to each other. Now and then we all feel a little lost and hurting, and this knowledge can be its own enlightenment.

To illustrate this point, I share a story I wrote many years ago:

A man needed to begin a journey, but the day had turned to night and he feared to begin. Unsure what to do, the man turned to a sage in the community.

"Take someone with you," counseled the teacher.

"But," moaned the man, "if I do that, then there will be two blind men on the path."

"No," said the teacher. "When two people discover each other's blindness, it is already growing light."

We all can get blindsided by life, and we all have a blind side. We can all also be a source of light to one another when we light candles of Humility, Honesty, Love and Faith. If this sounds simple, then let us simply do it.

The Compass for Healing can be used by children of any age. It can be used to protect the child within any of us. It can be used to help heal the child within who is in pain.

The Compass for Healing can be taught to anyone, but the best people to do that teaching are those who are trying to live by the Compass and use it to find their own way.

This is especially important for parents because children don't listen to their parents as much as they watch them. Make the stars on the Compass your ally and your children will adopt your ally.

_____

Children first look up to
their parents, then down at them
and finally at them.

_____

People learn 10 percent of what they read, 20 percent of what they hear, 30 percent of what they see, 50 percent of what they see and hear, 70 percent of what is discussed with others, 80 percent of what they experience, but 95 percent of what they teach to others.

Not only can you teach others about the Compass for Healing, the Compass will in fact impart its greatest lessons of strength to you when you care enough to pass its helping hand along.

When we pass on a good word, the good is on our lips and in our hearts. And we are strengthened.

Over a lifetime, most of us don't know our path is a path until we look back and see a lifetime of decisions meeting a lifetime of events.

It is my prayer that, on your path and with this Compass, you will be strengthened and be a source of strength to others.

"In the depth of winter, I finally learned that within me there lay an invincible summer."

—Albert Camus

About the Author

Noah benShea is one of North America's most respected and beloved public philosophers and the international bestselling author of twenty books translated into eighteen languages, including the beloved Jacob the Baker series, which is embraced around the world. In addition, he is noted as a scholar, theologian, executive advisor and renowned inspirational keynote speaker. His essays for the *New York Times* Regional Syndicate were nominated for the Pulitzer Prize, and his work has been included in publications of Oxford University Press, the Congressional Record and the World Bible Society in Jerusalem.

Widely interviewed by all the media and having served as Philosopher in Residence for numerous organizations, Noah benShea's "thoughts" that touch lives and stir conversation have also been branded by corporations as notable and diverse as American Greetings, Lucky Brand Jeans, Sugar Foods and Starbucks Coffee.

He was an Assistant Dean of Students at UCLA by the age of twenty-two and by thirty had been a "Fellow" at several think tanks, including the esteemed Center for the Study of Democratic Institutions in Santa Barbara, and the Center for the Humanities at the University of Southern California.

Born in Toronto, Mr. benShea has lived in Santa Barbara for over thirty years. He is the father of a daughter, Jordan, and a son, Adam, and is married to Julia Mora an interior designer. Visit him at www.NoahbenShea.com.

Waking Your

Dreams

Unlock the *Wisdom* of Your Unconscious

Discover your personal imagery.
Meet your authentic self.
Explore beneath the surface of your mind.

Emma Mellon, Ph.D.

Code #5547 • Paperback • $14.95

Discover the hidden messages in your dreams.

DR. JOE DISPENZA
As featured in the hit movie
What the Bleep Do We Know!?

EVOLVE
your
BRAIN

The Science of Changing Your Mind

Code #480X • Hardcover • $24.95

Cutting-edge research shows you how to stop negative patterns and break bad habits.